Truckload of Sky:
The Lost Songs of
David McComb
Vol. 1

33 1/3 Global

33 1/3 Global, a series related to but independent from **33 1/3**, takes the format of the original series of short, music-based books and brings the focus to music throughout the world. With initial volumes focusing on Japanese and Brazilian music, the series will also include volumes on the popular music of Australia/Oceania, Europe, Africa, the Middle East, and more.

33 1/3 Japan

Series Editor: Noriko Manabe

Spanning a range of artists and genres – from the 1970s rock of Happy End to technopop band Yellow Magic Orchestra, the Shibuya-kei of Cornelius, classic anime series *Cowboy Bebop*, J-Pop/EDM hybrid Perfume, and vocaloid star Hatsune Miku – 33 1/3 Japan is a series devoted to in-depth examination of Japanese popular music of the twentieth and twenty-first centuries.

Published Titles:

Supercell's *Supercell* by Keisuke Yamada

AKB48 by Patrick W. Galbraith and Jason G. Karlin

Yoko Kanno's *Cowboy Bebop Soundtrack* by Rose Bridges

Perfume's *Game* by Patrick St. Michel

Cornelius's *Fantasma* by Martin Roberts

Joe Hisaishi's *My Neighbor Totoro: Soundtrack* by Kunio Hara

Shonen Knife's *Happy Hour* by Brooke McCorkle Okazaki

Nenes' *Koza Dabasa* by Henry Johnson

Yuming's *The 14th Moon* by Lasse Lehtonen

Toshiko Akiyoshi-Lew Tabackin Big Band's *Kogun* by E. Taylor Atkins

S.O.B.'s *Don't Be Swindle* by Mahon Murphy and Ran Zwigenberg

Forthcoming Titles:

Kohaku Utagassen: The Red and White Song Contest by Shelley Brunt

Yellow Magic Orchestra's *Yellow Magic Orchestra* by Toshiyuki Ohwada

33 1/3 Brazil

Series Editor: Jason Stanyek

Covering the genres of samba, tropicália, rock, hip hop, forró, bossa nova, heavy metal and funk, among others, 33 1/3 Brazil is a series devoted to in-depth examination of the most important Brazilian albums of the twentieth and twenty-first centuries.

Published Titles:

Caetano Veloso's *A Foreign Sound* by Barbara Browning

Tim Maia's *Tim Maia Racional Vols. 1 &2* by Allen Thayer

João Gilberto and Stan Getz's *Getz/Gilberto* by Brian McCann

Gilberto Gil's *Refazenda* by Marc A. Hertzman

Dona Ivone Lara's *Sorriso Negro* by Mila Burns

Milton Nascimento and Lô Borges's *The Corner Club* by Jonathon Grasse

Racionais MCs' *Sobrevivendo no Inferno* by Derek Pardue

Naná Vasconcelos's *Saudades* by Daniel B. Sharp

Chico Buarque's First *Chico Buarque* by Charles A. Perrone

Forthcoming titles:

Jorge Ben Jor's *África Brasil* by Frederick J. Moehn

33 1/3 Europe

Series Editor: Fabian Holt

Spanning a range of artists and genres, 33 1/3 Europe offers engaging accounts of popular and culturally significant albums of Continental Europe and the North Atlantic from the twentieth and twenty-first centuries.

Published Titles:

Darkthrone's *A Blaze in the Northern Sky* by Ross Hagen

Ivo Papazov's *Balkanology* by Carol Silverman

Heiner Müller and Heiner Goebbels's *Wolokolamsker Chaussee* by Philip V. Bohlman

Modeselektor's *Happy Birthday!* by Sean Nye

Mercyful Fate's *Don't Break the Oath* by Henrik Marstal

Bea Playa's *I'll Be Your Plaything* by Anna Szemere and András Rónai

Various Artists' *DJs do Guetto* by Richard Elliott

Czesław Niemen's *Niemen Enigmatic* by Ewa Mazierska and Mariusz Gradowski

Massada's *Astaganaga* by Lutgard Mutsaers

Los Rodriguez's *Sin Documentos* by Fernán del Val and Héctor Fouce

Édith Piaf's *Récital 1961* by David Looseley

Nuovo Canzoniere Italiano's *Bella Ciao* by Jacopo Tomatis

Iannis Xenakis's *Persepolis* by Aram Yardumian

Vopli Vidopliassova's *Tantsi* by Maria Sonevytsky

Amália Rodrigues's *Amália at the Olympia* by Lila Ellen Gray

Ardit Gjebrea's *Projekt Jon* by Nicholas Tochka

Aqua's *Aquarium* by C.C. McKee

J.M.K.E.'s *To the Cold Land* by Brigitta Davidjants

Taco Hemingway's *Jarmark* by Kamila Rymajdo

Einstürzende Neubauten's *Kollaps* by Melle Jan Kromhout and Jan Nieuwenhuis

Forthcoming Titles:

Tripes' *Kefali Gemato Hrisafi* by Dafni Tragaki

Silly's *Februar* by Michael Rauhut

CCCP's *Fedeli Alla Linea's 1964–1985 Affinità-Divergenze Fra Il Compagno Togliatti E Noi Del Conseguimento Della Maggiore Età* by Giacomo Bottà

Sigur Rós' *Ágætis Byrjun* by Tore Størvold

33 1/3 Oceania

Series Editors: Jon Stratton (senior editor) and Jon Dale (specializing in books on albums from Aotearoa/New Zealand)

Spanning a range of artists and genres from Australian Indigenous artists to Maori and Pasifika artists, from Aotearoa/New Zealand noise music to Australian rock, and including music from Papua and other Pacific islands, 33 1/3 Oceania offers exciting accounts of albums that illustrate the wide range of music made in the Oceania region.

Published Titles:
John Farnham's *Whispering Jack* by Graeme Turner
The Church's *Starfish* by Chris Gibson
Regurgitator's *Unit* by Lachlan Goold and Lauren Istvandity
Kylie Minogue's *Kylie* by Adrian Renzo and Liz Giuffre
Alastair Riddell's *Space Waltz* by Ian Chapman
Hunters & Collectors's *Human Frailty* by Jon Stratton
The Front Lawn's *Songs from the Front Lawn* by Matthew Bannister
Bic Runga's *Drive* by Henry Johnson
The Dead C's *Clyma est mort* by Darren Jorgensen
Ed Kuepper's *Honey Steel's Gold* by John Encarnacao
Chain's *Toward the Blues* by Peter Beilharz
Hilltop Hoods' *The Calling* by Dianne Rodger
Screamfeeder's *Kitten Licks* by Ben Green and Ian Rogers
The Clean's *Boodle Boodle Boodle* by Geoff Stahl
The Avalanches' *Since I Left You* by Charles Fairchild
John Sangster's *Lord of the Rings Vols. 1-3* by Bruce Johnson
Soundtrack from *Saturday Night Fever* by Clinton Walker
Eyeliner's *BUY NOW* by Michael Brown
TISM's *Machiavelli and the Four Seasons* by Tyler Jenke
Crowded House's *Together Alone* by Barnaby Smith
silverchair's *Frogstomp* by Jay Daniel Thompson
Various Artists' *Truckload of Sky: The Lost Songs of David McComb Vol. 1*
by Glenn D'Cruz

Forthcoming Titles:
The Triffids' *Born Sandy Devotional* by Christina Ballico
5MMM's *Compilation Album of Adelaide Bands 1980* by Collette
Snowden
INXS' *Kick* by Lauren Moxey
Sunnyboys' *Sunnyboys* by Stephen Bruel
The La De Das' *The Happy Prince* by John Tebbutt
Gary Shearston's *Dingo* by Peter Mills
Kate Ceberano's *Brave* by Panizza Allmark
Robert Forster's *Danger in the Past* by Patrick Chapman

Dinah Lee's *Introducing Dinah Lee* by Kimberly Cannady
The Waifs' *Up All Night* by Rebecca Bennison
The Three Out's *Move* by James Gaunt
Split Enz' *Mental Notes* by Michael Lamb
Tame Impala's *Currents* by Alister Newstead

33 1/3 South Asia

Series Editor: Natalie Sarrazin

From the films of Bollywood and Lollywood, to home-grown *bhangra* hip-hop, Hindu devotional pop and Sufi rock, Sri Lankan rap, Indo jazz and disco, new-wave electronica and diasporic Asian Underground scene, 33 1/3 South Asia takes readers on a sonically diverse journey through the most significant soundtracks and albums from the twentieth and twenty-first centuries.

Published:
Dil Chahta Hai Soundtrack by Jayson Beaster-Jones
Lata Mangeshkar's *My Favourites, Volume 2* by Anirudha Bhattacharjee and Chandrashekhar Rao
Coke Studio (Season 14) by Rakae Rehman Jamil and Khadija Muzaffar

33 1/3 Africa

Series Editor: Michael Veal

33 1/3 Africa is a series of books on canonical, album-length works of African music including traditional music, experimental music, and, with particular emphasis, popular music. Academic and journalistic writing results in sophisticated, nuanced and accessible narratives on African music.

Published:
Fela Anikulapo-Kuti's *Sorrow Tears and Blood* by Stephanie Shonekan

Forthcoming Titles:
Cesária Évora's *Miss Perfumado* by Jacqueline Georgis
Paul Simon's *Graceland* by Kalvin Schmidt-Rimpler Dinh
Nico, Rochereau, Roger & L'African Fiesta – *Volume 1 (1962–1963)* by Frank Gunderson

Truckload of Sky: The Lost Songs of David McComb Vol. 1

Glenn D'Cruz

Series Editor: Jon Stratton, UniSA Creative, University of South Australia, and Jon Dale, University of Melbourne, Australia

BLOOMSBURY ACADEMIC

NEW YORK • LONDON • OXFORD • NEW DELHI • SYDNEY

BLOOMSBURY ACADEMIC
Bloomsbury Publishing Inc, 1385 Broadway, New York, NY 10018, USA
Bloomsbury Publishing Plc, 50 Bedford Square, London, WC1B 3DP, UK
Bloomsbury Publishing Ireland, 29 Earlsfort Terrace, Dublin 2, D02 AY28, Ireland

BLOOMSBURY, BLOOMSBURY ACADEMIC and the Diana logo are trademarks
of Bloomsbury Publishing Plc

First published in the United States of America 2025

Library of Congress Cataloging-in-Publication Data
Names: D'Cruz, Glenn, author.
Title: Truckload of sky : the lost songs of David McComb / Glenn D'Cruz.
Description: New York : Bloomsbury Academic, 2025. |
Series: 33 1/3 Oceania | Includes bibliographical references and index. |
Summary: "A Truckload of Sky: The Lost Songs of David McComb (2020) was
written by McComb and recorded by his friends and musical collaborators after
his untimely death at age 36 in 1999. McComb's songwriting is notable for its
erudite, poetic lyrics which are married to haunting melodies that evoke the
tumult and disorientations generated by love. Here, a hauntological approach is
used to unpack the album's structure and composition. This book examines the
ways A Truckload of Sky echoes McComb's stylistic and thematic obsessions
while generating important questions about the relationship between popular
music and memory, time and death"– Provided by publisher.
Identifiers: LCCN 2025002968 | ISBN 9798765127469 | ISBN 9798765127452 |
ISBN 9798765127476 | ISBN 9798765127483
Subjects: LCSH: McComb, David, 1962-1999. Truckload of sky. |
McComb, David, 1962-1999–Criticism and interpretation. |
Popular music–Australia–History and criticism.
Classification: LCC ML420.M34117 D37 2025 |
DDC 782.42164092–dc23/eng/20250123
LC record available at https://lccn.loc.gov/2025002968

ISBN: HB: 979-8-7651-2745-2
            PB: 979-8-7651-2746-9
          ePDF: 979-8-7651-2748-3
         eBook: 979-8-7651-2747-6

Series: 33 1/3 Oceania

Typeset by Integra Software Services Pvt. Ltd.
Printed and bound in the United States of America

For product safety related questions contact productsafety@bloomsbury.com.

To find out more about our authors and books visit www.bloomsbury.com and
sign up for our newsletters.

Contents

Acknowledgements

Thanks to Graham Lee, Robert McComb and J. P. Shilo for taking the time to speak to me about their contributions to *Truckload of Sky* and answering my questions about their creative process. Thanks also to Jon Stratton for his editorial input and valuable scholarship on the Perth music scene. Thanks to Sonia Sankovich for her enduring support and encouragement. Special thanks to Leonard D'Cruz for his insightful comments on my manuscript and his helpful editorial suggestions. Thanks, finally, to David McComb for his peerless catalogue of songs.

Preface

I fell in love with The Triffids on a scorching summer afternoon in 1983. The band played on the back of a flatbed truck in the middle of James Street, Northbridge. My parched mouth and burning skin told me I should find some shade, but I sat, transfixed, cross-legged, immobilized, on the hot bitumen road, which had been closed off to traffic to accommodate the music festival crowd. I shielded my eyes from the blazing sun with my hands as I craned my head to get a better view of the band. Yes, this felt like the real thing. Some musical loves do not endure. You look back on them as you might recollect a one-night stand that filled you with a rush of excitement before ending in disappointment and disgust. I'll refrain from naming names, but there's more than one Mancunian band whose collected works I took to the thrift shop after a few years. My love for The Triffids and my emotional investment in their music have endured. This book is a testament to my unwavering commitment to their legacy.

Love at first sight? I can't be sure. Episodic memory is notoriously unreliable (Sacks, 2008, 220). Prior to that memorable day, I'd seen The Triffids perform a few pub gigs. I was aware of the band's songwriter and lead singer, David McComb, since he was a fellow student of mine at the Western Australian Institute of Technology (WAIT) – we attended the same photojournalism class for a few months in 1981. David struck me as an affable, intelligent classmate, but I was oblivious to his talent as a songwriter.

With his trademark neckerchief and slender frame, David mesmerized the assembled crowd as he strummed his acoustic twelve-string guitar. Most of the onlookers were casual visitors, delighting in the vibrant atmosphere beneath the vast expanse of blue sky that enveloped the city. On this occasion, the band favoured their folky ballads over the more raucous numbers in their repertoire. The rhythm section – Alsy MacDonald on drums and Martyn Casey on bass – played synchronized beats, sometimes in waltz-time. David's brother, Robert, alternated between electric guitar and violin, imbuing the tunes with delicate textures, drones and fills. The band's keyboard player, Jill Birt, added simple counter-melodies and washes of sustained chords, which gave the songs an ethereal quality. The Triffids sounded confident, majestic and distinctive, contrasting with the blues and boogie bands that dominated that day's program (I recall Midget and the Farrellys revving up the inebriated crowd later that day, but I have no distinct memories of the other festival participants).

I found David's music appealing, despite being unfamiliar with most of the tunes in The Triffids' set that day. The songs were melodic and hooky, devoid of fat. These tunes were trimmed of excess flamboyance – no flashy guitar solos, boogie rhythms or vocal gymnastics. And the lyrics were intelligent, literary, often referencing Perth itself. Songs like 'Too Hot to Move', 'Spanish Blue' and 'Hell of a Summer' were made for such a day, resonating with the summer festival's ambience. I was hooked. From that point on The Triffids became an integral part of my youth, playing a pivotal role in my social life (as I became more involved with Perth's small alternative music culture) and providing the soundtrack to subsequent rites of passage, especially those connected with matters of the heart.

David's death in 1999 hit me as hard as losing a close friend. Listening to his albums in the aftermath of his tragic demise was revelatory. On reflection, my early passion for his work had as much to do with the spirit of the alternative 1980s as it did with the music itself (I will always associate The Triffids with an especially formative and joyful period of my life). But my appreciation for David's music deepened after his passing, as I became more aware of his singular genius and his significant contribution to Australian popular music and literary culture. I know I can never disconnect my personal associations from my assessment of David McComb's music and proffer a dispassionate account of his oeuvre, which is why I have steered into the skid and combined scholarship with personal reflections. I hope this slim volume conveys my sincere admiration for David McComb's art and contributes to the growing body of literature devoted to his towering talent.

Introduction: Archives, affects, ethics

Truckload of Sky: The Lost Songs of David McComb arrived via mail order during the first months of the COVID pandemic in 2020. During Melbourne's lockdowns, I played the album obsessively. I was struck by the quality of the songwriting on the record, and by the uncanny presence of McComb's writing voice, which was filtered through the performances of a diverse group of singers. Commenting on a rehearsal he witnessed for the recording, Michael Dwyer, arts journalist for *The Age*, observed that 'no matter who was singing, it was McComb's voice that filled the room. It's a voice of cruel, knowing truths with no time to guild them, heavy with scripture and poetry and plangent chords that seem to lunge at an infinite sky' (2020).

The album is, in effect, McComb's second solo record.[1] As a long-standing fan, listening to *Truckload of Sky* felt unsettling. It was like receiving an unexpected gift from a lost friend, or a ghost. I found the album compelling for two reasons. First, it fractured my already-fragile sense of temporality (due to being locked down for months) by opening portals into the

---

[1]   McComb released his first solo record, *Love of Will*, in 1994. The album remains unavailable on CD or vinyl, but it is available on most major streaming platforms such as Spotify, Apple Music and Tidal.

past. Memories of people and places I hadn't thought about for decades became vivid, prompting me to reckon with the spirit of another time. Second, it motivated me to investigate McComb's music more critically.

I asked myself the following questions: what is distinctive about his songwriting? Does his body of work transcend nostalgia for Australian alternative music in the 1980s? What does McComb's career tell us about Australian popular culture in the latter part of the twentieth century? Why has his reputation as one of Australia's best songwriters grown since his death? To what extent is he a quintessentially Australian writer?

This book aims to answer these questions by describing and analyzing McComb's historical and cultural context. It also seeks to provide readers with a deeper understanding of the factors that shaped his artistic sensibility. It does this by using his songs as prompts to generate commentaries on topics including McComb's attitudes towards Perth and its music culture and the role urban and rural spaces play in his oeuvre. Through archival research and interviews with some of the musicians who produced *Truckload of Sky*, the second half of the book also tells the story of how McComb's friends, family and fans have kept his artistic legacy alive. Because the story of McComb's life and the creation of the album both deal with subjects such as mortality, memory, loss, presence and absence, the perspective I take in this book is shaped by the notion of hauntology.

Like many fans of McComb and The Triffids, I have been 'haunted' by his songs for most of my adult life in the sense that his music insistently plays in my head during moments of emotional turmoil. However, *Truckload of Sky* also prompted me to think about the experience of being haunted by music in a more complex way. The novelist DBC Pierre wrote he is 'haunted' by the music of The Triffids, which exists 'out of time'. Indeed, it is this atemporal quality that he finds distinctive and compelling. The band, he suggests, deliberately rejected the trappings of mainstream 1980s culture, in terms of sonics, image and attitude.

For Pierre, The Triffids are emblematic of a social stratum (an educated, affluent class) that has lost its innocence and faith in dominant cultural myths about the so-called 'lucky country'. This may be true, but why does he say he is *haunted* by the band's music? He used the word as a verb, suggesting that he frequently feels compelled to return to the band's records because they unsettle the conventional picture of Australian culture in the 1980s. I share this perspective to some degree. Indeed, I feel an odd disconnect when I see images from the 1980s. I don't recall people wearing so much hair gel, spandex and neon colours. Fans of alternative music were generally clad in black. I don't recall too many women rocking voluminous poodle hair styles or wearing shoulder pads in the venues that hosted post-punk music (not that fans of bands like The Triffids didn't embrace aspects of 1980s fashions). The key point, I think, is that the common signifiers of 1980s popular culture mask a more complex and heterogeneous reality. Pierre is haunted by another world—one that existed alongside the electric blue razzle and lime green sparkle of the era.

The word 'haunted' carries sinister connotations, even when used to convey one's obsession with a particular thing or person. Like Pierre, I'm haunted by the music of The Triffids, but in a more personal sense. The band, as I have already noted, played a formative role in my private life. Their music provided the backdrop for significant and insignificant moments and milestones. When I hear a song by The Triffids, it's as though I experience aspects of the past in the present. Nostalgia, in the everyday sense of the word, plays a role in my personal enjoyment of the band's music. And this is reason enough for readers to be cautious about the claims I make in this book about the cultural significance of McComb's songs. Am I not just indulging in nostalgia for my youth? The answer to this question has to be a resounding yes, which is precisely why I feel it's important to unpack my response to *Truckload of Sky* through the lens of hauntology, which compels us to engage with the figure of the ghost in a manner that yields a more sober account of McComb's legacy and his context.

If this volume was not part of a series, I might have called it *Spectres of David McComb*, after Derrida's seminal book, *Spectres of Marx* (1994) since the concept of *hauntology*, coined by Derrida and developed in another direction by Mark Fisher, functions as a subtle guiding thread for my commentary on *Truckload of Sky*.[2] Derrida's neologism, 'Hauntology' [*hantologie*], is based on a pun in French, as it is pronounced like the French word for 'ontology' [*ontologie*]. Ontology is the branch of philosophy concerned with Being – with what *it is to be*. For Derrida, the term undermines the common-sense assumption that the present is self-sufficient. Hauntology also refers to the way virtual, immaterial forces shape our existence. It has implications for thinking about how we engage with the dead (who continue to commune with the living in a variety of ways). This second sense of the term, which owes more to Derrida than Fisher, generates a series of philosophical questions about identity and friendship, which I address through my commentary on McComb's songs.

---

[2] Inspired by Derrida (1994), Fisher's concept of hauntology explores the lingering presence of lost futures in popular culture, a kind of ghostly persistence of what could have been (2012; 2014; 2016).

The language of hauntology and the figure of the ghost also provide a useful way to engage with *Truckload of Sky* for a more specific reason: McComb's best songs, as we shall see, are mysterious. Hauntology and mystery are deeply intertwined. Both concepts deal with the elusive, the intangible, and the unsettling. Hauntology evokes a temporal mystery – time becomes non-linear, with echoes of the past 'haunting' the present and reshaping the future. This temporal ambiguity is inherently mysterious, as it resists simple explanation or resolution.

McComb believed in the power of mystery. Graham Lee, a member of The Triffids, recalls that McComb once said

> mystery is the most important element in a song. If it doesn't contain mystery, it's not a complete song. This is why he preferred 'Would You Lay with Me (In a Field of Stone)?' to 'Waterloo Sunset'. The king of mystery left plenty behind in his songs and in the lives of those who were touched by the music or the man.
>
> (2009, 159)

The word 'mystery' suggests something that is inexplicable or difficult to understand. I agree with Lee that McComb's best songs are mysterious. However, they're also unsettling and, yes, haunting.

In this book, I revisit themes that I previously explored in my book *Hauntological Dramaturgy* (2022). However, this present work delves into a more comprehensive analysis of David McComb's songwriting, which was only briefly discussed in one chapter of my previous book that primarily focused on theatrical performance. There are three major topics that organize my thinking in both works: affects, archives and ethics.

Affects

I began an earlier draft of this book with the sentence: 'David McComb's songs always made me think.' This is a true enough statement. His lyrics contain thoughtful insights into romantic relationships and the ineffable forces that shape our emotional lives. On further reflection, though, I must concede I was first attracted to his music by the way it made me *feel*, the way it affected my state of Being. For me, The Triffids, at their best, produced *mood* music. I use the word 'mood', after Heidegger, to refer to an integral aspect of human Being, a fundamental *existentiale* in Heidegger's vocabulary (1962, 172–3). Heidegger claims that we always have some kind of mood; we are always attuned to aspects of the world (the weather, the landscape, objects and so on) which mood discloses. I will address this topic with specific reference to The Triffids' status as a 'landscape' band, but I first want to frame my discussion of the affective qualities of McComb's music with a personal anecdote.

While mesmerized by McComb's live performances, which became increasingly dramatic over the years, I don't think I connected with the emotional force of his music fully until one day, towards the end of 1987, I was driving my beat-up blue Mazda, heading to a shitty dead-end job, when 'Wide Open Road' came on the car radio. I felt a nauseating lump rise in my throat. Overwhelmed, I pulled the 'blue bomb' over to the side of the road and sobbed. There wasn't a cloud in the sky. It was a bright summer's day in Perth, yet the song transformed my environment and put me in touch with a disturbing sense of loss. Until that point, I'd been able to pretend that my ex-girlfriend hadn't left me, that my job was meaningful, that I was getting my shit together. McComb's song disclosed despair as an integral aspect of the world. This shift in mood attuned me to the unpleasant dimensions of my situation. Such is the affective power of music.[3]

Undoubtedly, my emotional attachment to The Triffids' music has played a crucial role in creating this book. Consequently, I have tried to blend scholarly sobriety with personal enthusiasm. While this strategy is open to accusations of self-indulgence, reflecting on our affective engagement with art can be a valuable source of autoethnographic knowledge. It can function as a supplement to materialist analyses of institutions and discourses. Rita Felski points out that academic protocols can disguise the ways our emotional investment in our objects of study shapes our research questions. Indeed, an undue emphasis on 'objective' scholarly procedures 'screens out any flicker of emotion, tamps down idiosyncratic impulses, and steers clear of the first-person voice' (2015, 48).[4]

Archives

David McComb chronicled his life, particularly his creative journey, through journals, diaries, and notebooks brimming with production notes, lists, letters, postcards. Crucially, his personal archive also included demo recordings of his songs. Bleddyn Butcher threads these primary sources into a

---

[3] It is important to note that not everybody experiences music in this way. Oliver Sacks has documented the phenomenon known as Amusia, which prevents some people from having any affective response to music (Sacks, 2008, 120).

[4] Cultural Studies scholars regularly address the relationship between affects and personal taste. See Frith (1996) and Wilson (2014) for examples of this topic with reference to the study of popular music.

rich, compelling narrative that captures evocative strands of McComb's personal and professional world, along with the spirit of the 1980s independent music scene. Similarly, Jonathan Alley has drawn from this personal archive, which includes photographs and 8 mm film alongside the written material, to craft a feature-length documentary about McComb's life. We can also think of the *Truckload of Sky* album as an archival project or, more accurately, as an 'anarchival' practice, where the fragments of McComb's life are reassembled for creative exploration.[5] The archives of artists of all kinds, whether dead or alive, are valuable commodities. We live in an era where outtakes, demos and unreleased songs are re-packaged, often in lavish box sets or other formats, to meet a commercial demand for more product. Artists from the 'Baby Boomer' generation, most notably The Beatles, Bob Dylan and Neil Young, regularly mine their vaults for 'rare' material.

Digital technology has also made it possible to 'collaborate' with dead artists. For example, de-mixing technology facilitated The Beatles' 'last' track, 'Now and Then', by enabling surviving members of the band to turn a rough John Lennon demo into a polished recording. Examples of dead artists returning as holograms or avatars are legion: Tupac Shakur 'returned from the dead' as part of Snoop Dog's performance at the 2012 Coachella Valley Music & Arts Festival, and ABBA, whose members are all still living at the time of writing, perform as avatars (using motion capture technology) in their 'ABBA Voyage' show. The fascination with outtakes, demos,

---

5   Brian Massumi, among others, uses the term 'anarchival' to signal those practices that use the archive as an inspiration for creative practice as opposed to a repository of static artefacts (2016).

and unreleased recordings by musicians is symptomatic of a broader cultural interest in archives.

One key concept in understanding this obsession is Walter Benjamin's idea of the 'aura' of an artwork, which he discusses in 'The Work of Art in the Age of Mechanical Reproduction' (1973). Benjamin argues original works of art have a unique presence or aura tied to their authenticity and rarity. Fans often perceive demos and unreleased recordings as more 'authentic' because they offer an unpolished version of the artist's creative process, unmediated by the ornaments and gloss of a realized production. Nick Hornby's novel, *Juliet Naked* (2009), satirizes this often-obsessive practice amongst music fans.

This desire to access the raw, rare, or unadorned is a form of what Derrida calls 'archive fever'. To be stricken with this affliction 'is to have compulsive, repetitive, and nostalgic desire for the archive, an irrepressible desire to return to the origin, a homesickness, a nostalgia for the return to the most archaic place of absolute commencement' (Derrida, 1996, 91).

The archive is also a haunted space in Fisher's formulation of hauntology since archival objects (such as forgotten audio-visual recordings) can be re-purposed to evoke a sense of what could have been. He develops this theme by exploring how popular music, especially electronic and post-punk, recycles sounds and styles from past eras to remind us of those 'lost futures' that represent alternatives to the cultural and political present. Artists like Burial, Boards of Canada and others associated with the Ghost Box label combine archival recordings with contemporary production techniques to evoke a sense of temporal dislocation. These artists create music that is 'critically nostalgic', reflecting Fisher's view that hauntology is about the affective experience of a future that feels both inevitable and impossible.

The artists that came to be labelled hauntological were suffused with an overwhelming melancholy; and they were preoccupied with the way in which technology materialised memory – hence a fascination with television, vinyl records, audiotape, and with the sounds of these technologies breaking down. This fixation on materialised memory led to what is perhaps the principal sonic signature of hauntology: the use of crackle, the surface noise made by vinyl.

(Fisher, 2014, 19)

While Fisher uses the concept of hauntology to commune with the various ghosts of his past (which include bands like The Fall, Joy Division and Japan and various films and TV shows), it is too easy to equate hauntology with a specific genre. The concept, as this book shows, applies to a wider range of music that uses archival material.

There is another more personal dimension to our relation to archives. Performance Studies scholar, Heike Roms, distinguishes between the concept of the archive as a singular, authoritative institution tied to power structures, and the dynamic, creative nature of archival practices. These practices – such as selecting, sorting, classifying, preserving and managing materials – shape (through the collections we maintain, curate and understand) artistic legacies (Roms, 2013, 38). Roms highlights how various groups, including scholars, artists and archivists, *care* for the legacies of performers and productions held in institutions like galleries, libraries and museums. As we will see in subsequent chapters, friends and families also contribute to preserving the memories of the deceased. Significantly, the *Truckload of Sky* liner notes credit 'the *friends of David McComb*'[my emphasis] as the group responsible for making the record, which is why I frame my account of the making of the album with questions about friendship.

Ethics

There is an ethical aspect to all these interconnected archival practices since they involve a duty of care towards the absent artist. This is especially true for those projects that involve a deceased public figure such as David McComb. I don't see *Truckload of Sky* as just a tribute to McComb (the album contains unknown songs for starters). The makers of the album describe it as a 'labour of love' but express caution in their approach to realizing McComb's 'lost' songs. Would he approve of the album's instrumentation, the choice of singers, the arrangements, even the choice of material? Of course, there is no way to know what McComb may have thought about his lost songs being recorded so long after his death. How should we honour his wishes, given that he left no explicit instructions about how to produce his unfinished works? In what ways could McComb's friends' obligations to him evolve as time passes or social and political situations shift? Does art transcend all ethical considerations, as Oscar Wilde once suggested (2003)?[6] And what of Emmanuel Levinas' insistence that existence compels us to respond to and be responsible for the other (1969)? Derrida's concept of hauntology resonates with Levinas' ethics, yet, as scholars like Martin Hägglund (2008, 78) argue, Derrida also recognizes that every ethical decision involves an inescapable violence – exclusion or erasure that is intrinsic to pursuing justice.

Despite these deeper philosophical entanglements, the primary focus here remains on the practical aspects of creating performances that engage with spirits and spectres, rather than an exhaustive investigation into these ethical considerations

---

[6]   Wilde's book was originally published in 1891.

which we cannot resolve. As we shall see, my conversations with some friends of David McComb show they considered these ethical dilemmas as they wrestled with the practicalities of making *Truckload of Sky*.

*

Unlike most volumes in this series, this book is about a relatively unknown album. Its obscurity demands that I provide, at the outset, some justification for why it deserves a book-length study. Since its release in 2020, *Truckload of Sky: The Lost Songs of David McComb* has sold a few thousand copies and attracted scant critical attention; the few published reviews of the work have been thoughtful and enthusiastic, but they are too brief to provide an extensive appreciation of how this collection of songs illuminates McComb's career and creative oeuvre. This book seeks to correct this situation by filling a gap in critical commentary.

First, McComb is one of Australia's most celebrated songwriters, although critical acclaim in his own country was sparse during his lifetime. Several influential music critics recognized the quality of The Triffids' music during the band's heyday, but McComb's reputation has grown over the years. Since his premature death at the age of thirty-six, McComb's admirers, which include notable academics such as Niall Lucy, Claire Colebrook and John Kinsella, have written essays about his life and work. Bleddyn Butcher wrote a detailed biography of McComb in 2011. Fremantle Press published an anthology of writing about McComb, *Vagabond Holes* (2009) and a posthumous collection of his poetry, *Beautiful Waste: The Poems of David McComb* (2009). In 2007, SBS television commissioned a documentary on The Triffids' album *Born Sandy Devotional* (1986) as part of their *Great Australian Albums* series. More recently, Jonathan Alley directed a feature-length documentary film about McComb's life, *Love in Bright Landscapes: The Story of David McComb of The Triffids* (2020).

These works attest to McComb's status as an important writer whose work, besides possessing enduring literary and musical merit, played a formative role in shaping aspects of Australian culture in the 1980s, especially in relation to what Clinton Walker calls the Australian post-punk independent underground (2021). So, while McComb may not be a household name, his reputation as a significant Australian artist merits further commentary; the album *Truckload of Sky* presents an opportunity to deepen our understanding of McComb's legacy, especially regarding his unreleased songs.

Second, *Truckload of Sky* shows that ill health did not diminish McComb's formidable strengths as a songwriter. Many of the 'lost' songs on the record are amongst his strongest and most affecting. The album, then, is much more than a tribute project. It is, I will argue in subsequent chapters, a valuable, if not a major, addition to McComb's oeuvre, which addresses and provides a fascinating insight into how he addressed some of his thematic obsessions (love, loss and mortality) towards the end of his life.

Finally, *Truckload of Sky* is an album that invites us to think about the complex relationships between memory and mourning. The album is credited to 'The Friends of David McComb'. Some of these friends, like his brother Robert, Graham Lee, Rob Snarski and Phil Kakulas, were musical collaborators. Others, like Angie Hart and Chris Abrahams, were part of the same independent music scene. Some contributors to the album never met McComb, but, as we shall see, had their own reasons for contributing to a project that keeps McComb's spirit alive and provides us with another opportunity to think about the concept of friendship.

In his liner notes for the album, Graham Lee writes that 'it's through his songs that David becomes most alive to us' (2020). This statement acts as another guiding thread for this book, which, in a general sense, is concerned with unpacking the practical and philosophical problems posed when the archive of an artist is curated after their death. Simon Reynolds wrote that 'a record really is a ghost: it's a trace of a musician's body, the after-imprint of breath and exertion. There's a parallel between the phonograph and the photograph: both are reality's death mask' (2012, 312). Anyone can conjure McComb's 'ghost' through his existing audio-visual recordings. His compelling baritone voice is absent from *Truckload of Sky*, yet his *spirit* suffuses every track.

Chapter outline

The book begins with two contextual chapters. These sections are essential to grasping why *Truckload of Sky* is such a compelling embodiment of McComb's spirit and distinctive writing voice. To fully appreciate the album's impact, we must identify the unique qualities of his songwriting and explore how his singular voice was shaped by his geographical and cultural environment. I've organized the first two chapters like annotated mixtapes. This is fitting since McComb gathered his eclectic musical interests on cassettes, which he gifted to friends and family throughout his life. The first mixtape chapter is a kind of biographical sketch. It summarizes McComb's career as a songwriter, identifying what I find distinctive about his body of work, focusing on his thematic and stylistic preoccupations. I unpack a single song from each of the various stages of McComb's musical life (from his teenage cassette recordings to his work with costar, his last band) often referring to how elements of these songs manifest in the tracks on *Truckload of Sky*.

Chapter 2 focuses on McComb's often ambivalent relationship with his hometown through the songs he wrote (directly and obliquely) about Perth and Western Australia at various stages of his career. It also contextualizes McComb's music through various commentaries on the Perth music scene in the 1980s and other more general observations about Australian culture during this era, including a brief discussion about Perth's 'inner-city scene', or its apparent lack of such a scene. This chapter also addresses the relationship between mood and place, referring to the scholarly commentary on McComb's relationship to Perth's 'inner city', suburbia and rural Western Australia (Cull, 2005; Stratton, 2007; Stratton, 2009; Trainer and Stratton, 2016). Our appreciation of 'So Good to Be Home', one of *Truckload of Sky's* highlights, is deepened by this discussion.

Chapter 3 adopts a journalistic register, describing the making of *Truckload of Sky* through interviews with three of the album's key contributors: Graham Lee, Robert McComb and J. P. Shilo. It also focuses on the ethical and musical challenges posed by the formidable task of turning McComb's mostly primitive cassette demos into fully realized professional recordings. I frame this section of the book with a few brief remarks on the concept of friendship since the album is obviously a labour of love.

Chapter 4 comprises a track-by-track analysis of the album. It analyses the music, unpacks the lyrics to each song and includes commentary on how the tracks explore and reprise McComb's interest in human relationships and metaphysical questions about life, love and loss. It pays particular attention to the way McComb's writing voice manifests in the performances of the singers on the album.

Chapter 5 provides a short summation of the book's major themes and argues that David's career followed the trajectory of the classic hero's quest. While listeners don't need my commentary, analysis and annotations to appreciate the songs on *Truckload of Sky*, I hope this work will enrich the reader's enjoyment of McComb's rich artistic legacy, particularly *Truckload of Sky*, which is as good as anything he produced in his short lifetime.

1 A David McComb mixtape

The Triffids formed in 1978 and recorded several cassettes and 7-inch singles between 1978 and 1983. During this period, they amended their personnel before settling on a stable line-up of David McComb on guitar and lead vocals; his brother, Rob, on guitar, violin and backing vocals; Martin Casey on bass; Jill Birt on keyboards and occasional lead vocals; and Alsy MacDonald on drums and backing vocals. This incarnation of the group recorded the band's first album, *Treeless Plain* (1983), the mini album, *Raining Pleasure* (1984) and the *Field of Glass* EP (1985).[1] Graham Lee joined the band (on lap steel, pedal steel, acoustic and electric guitars) in 1985 and played a key role in the group's second album, *Born Sandy Devotional* (*BSD*), a record many critics consider the band's masterpiece (D'Cruz, 2022; Snow, 1986; Sweeting, 1986). The band released *In the Pines* later that year. The Triffids signed with Island records, a major international label in 1987, releasing three further albums, *Calenture* (1987), *The Black Swan* (1989) and *Live in Stockholm* (1990) – with the final record released after their break-up in 1989. David McComb pursued various projects during the 1990s. He released a few singles with Adam Peters, co-founded The Blackeyed Susans

---

[1]   An Extended Play (EP) is a recording that contains more tracks than a single but fewer than an album. That said, *Raining Pleasure* (which contained seven tracks) is categorized as a mini-LP.

with Phil Kakulas and Rob Snarski, and released a solo album, *Love of Will* (1995). He was working on recordings with his last band, costar, before his death in 1999.

These are the bare facts of McComb's career. Readers who want a more detailed account of McComb's life can consult Bleddyn Butcher's biography of David McComb, *Save What You Can: The Day of The Triffids* (2011). Butcher uses McComb's journals, letters, postcards and interviews to construct a compelling account of his life. He often uses the technique of 'free indirect discourse' to tell McComb's story. In simple terms, this novelistic strategy expresses the first-person thoughts of a character through third-person narration, blurring the distinction between the writer and his subject (Stevenson, 1997). Butcher's book is essential reading for die-hard fans (I cite this indispensable book throughout this volume). However, at over 500 pages long, this exhaustive account of McComb's life (until the band's demise) is not for the casual reader. Wilson Neates penned a shorter version of The Triffids' story in his article 'The Days of The Triffids' (2006), featuring insights from Graham Lee and Robert McComb.

This chapter identifies the qualities that make McComb a distinctive songwriter. Think of it as an annotated mixtape, where each track offers a glimpse into a different aspect of his multifarious creative personality (which is why I have given each entry a descriptive title that identifies a key aspect of McComb's artistic personality). By analysing one exemplary song from each stage of his career, the chapter also functions as a biographical sketch. I also hope to convey, where appropriate, why the language of hauntology enriches our appreciation of McComb's songs. I've chosen tracks from his teenage years in the late 1970s to the poignant songs we wrote just before his death in 1999.

'Not the Marrying Kind' (1981 and 1984): The medium

In various early line-ups of The Triffids, McComb and his friends recorded seventy-nine songs on six cassette albums between May 1978 and April 1980 (Nichols, 2009, 79). McComb penned most of the material on the cassettes, which the band sold at gigs, and a few select independent record stores around Perth. 'Not the Marrying Kind' appears on tape six, the band's last cassette release, but I first heard a different version of the song on the *Lawson Square Infirmary* (*LSI*) 12-inch EP (1984). This latter version sounds like something Gram Parsons might have written. Whereas Graham Lee's dobro gives the *LSI* performance a convincing country feel, the cassette recording sounds like a cross between Phil Spector's production of 'Then He Kissed Me' by The Crystals and the bubble-gum/country songs Michael Nesmith recorded for The Monkees. McComb and Margaret Gillard (who played keyboards with this incarnation of the band) sing the chorus *a cappella* before the drums kick in with a beat borrowed from the Phil Spector track.

'Not the Marrying Kind' is about emotional detachment; the singer can, if he chooses, offer his paramour signs of affection (fancy food and drink) but remains emotionally distant and non-committal. Not only does the song's refrain suggest the singer finds his partner unsuitable (she drinks too much and talks 'double Dutch'), but it also reveals that he's not a regular guy. As a country music fan, I found the song appealing, but it's not the sort of tune post-punk bands often played. The song, in the present context, is notable for drawing attention to McComb's eclectic tastes. Indeed, one of McComb's great strengths as a writer was his refusal to commit to a single aesthetic, a proclivity that especially marked his work in the late 1980s and early 1990s but was evident in every stage of his career. Claire Colebrook puts this feature of McComb's work another way: 'The Triffids deployed a mode of "stratigraphic time," where all styles and possibilities were co-present (electronic and acoustic, harmonic and discordant, narrative and lyric, stylised and improvised)' (2009, 304).

The geological metaphor is apt since we apprehend rock sediments simultaneously. This disturbs simple temporal logic. This feature of McComb's writing will become clear as we progress through the following chapters. Without wanting to deny the affective power of music or those personal emotional experiences that inspire songwriting, I think the language of hauntology provides a better way of understanding the connections between tradition and individual talent, to borrow a phrase from T. S. Eliot (1932). It shows that historical consciousness involves temporal disjunction. That is an awareness of how the past and present co-exist. McComb's early compositions show his interest in learning from his forebears in pop music and, as we shall see, in literature.

Simon Reynolds calls the practice of seeing the artist as the sum of their influences as 'the portrait of the artist as a consumer' (2012, 171). So, rather than music coming from deep within, as in romanticism's spontaneous overflow of powerful feelings recollected in tranquillity (to paraphrase William Wordsworth), music is the sum of an artist's influences. I find the concept of 'influences' too prosaic. It smacks of a sober utilitarianism. I prefer to think of songwriting as a conversation with tradition, or a dialogue with ghosts. At its best, it's an artistic practice that involves an element of surrender to the *spirit* of music in the Nietzschean sense of the word. Indeed, it is only by surrendering to this spirit that the individual artist's ego dissolves into the collective and cosmic.[2]

I have written elsewhere about ventriloquism as a hauntological trope (D'Cruz, 2015); simply put, this is the unsettling affect generated when a listener discerns the stylistic traces of other artists in a new song. This apprehension disturbs the commonly held assumption that an artist is a self-sufficient entity (D'Cruz, 2015, 263).

'Influences' are spectral in the sense that singers, even in their original compositions, function as 'mediums' for the voices of others (although it is not always apparent if the singer animates the spirit, or the spirit animates the singer). As a serious and knowledgeable student of pop music history, McComb was not afraid to engage with tradition.

For example, it's easy to discern Lou Reed's 'influence' on David McComb in a song like 'Love and Affection' which uses the unmistakable chordal riff from 'Sweet Jane' or the way McComb uses non-sensible syllables, in the manner of 1960s girl groups and doo wop, in the backing vocals of songs like 'Hometown Farewell Kiss'. McComb's 'reference points' (as he called them) are legion: the extensive production notes he made for *Born Sandy Devotional* contain references to the string sounds on Leonard Cohen's 'Avalanche', the cymbal rolls

---

[2] Nietzsche believed that music embodies chaos, ecstasy and a direct connection to the raw, unmediated essence of life, symbolized by the figure of the Greek God, Dionysus, the OG rock star (1967, 20–2). Primal Dionysian energy contrasts with Apollonian structure, order and form. The music of The Triffids contains Dionysian and Apollonian elements. The band's use of idiosyncratic and atmospheric instrumentation articulates the ineffable through echoes, reverberations and ghostly sounds that complement McComb's evocative lyrics.

on Bowie's 'Jean Genie' the way Tom Waits uses a vibraphone on 'Swordfish Trombone', the vocal echo in Springsteen's 'State Trooper' among so many others. The mixtapes he made for friends show an even wider range of musical interests. For example, a tape from 1986 includes cuts from Al Green, Sly and The Family Stone, John Lee Hooker, Aretha Franklin and Bruce Springsteen alongside Richard Hell and The Birthday Party. Of course, it's not always possible to hear these reference sounds in actual recordings, but that's beside the point. McComb was obsessed with engaging with and repurposing sounds and production techniques that caught his attention.

On one level, writers regularly use 'reference points' or 'influences' as a point of departure for a new work. But songs belong to traditions and often use generic chords, scales, rhythms, instrumental techniques and so on. On a fundamental level, all songs connect with diverse cultural and musical traditions and serve as channels through which spectral voices can materialize in various forms and contexts.

'Place in the Sun' (1981, 1982, 1983): The craftsman

Most early Triffids' songs are earworms – carefully structured, hook-laden, pop gems. 'Place in the Sun' is a good example of the band's prowess as a pop band. The song appears on *Tape 6*, the *Reverie* EP and the band's debut album, *Treeless Plain*. Both non-album iterations begin with a simple guitar riff played with twelfth fret harmonics, followed by a strummed second guitar (which drops out of the mix as the song progresses); the bass then comes in with another riff while, underneath, a snare drum pattern builds in intensity, climaxing as the vocal propels the song forward. The tune blends specific instrumental lines into a captivating whole. This is nothing unusual; most good pop songs, especially those from the 1960s and 1970s, incorporate instrumental hooks and thoughtful arrangements. Whereas the tempo fluctuates in the 1981 and 1982 recordings, exposing the band's limitations during its early stage, the album version is polished and tight.

Dispensing with the instrumental introduction, McComb gets to the point with a commanding vocal that comes in with the music. The lyrics are about alienation. Fleeing from vulnerability and connection, the singer feels jaded and detached, resorting to physical escape, cynicism or self-imposed isolation. The narrator's message is bleak: no matter what choice you make, you'll never find your proper place in the order of things.

Despite developing a more atmospheric, cinematic style of songwriting, as he matured, McComb never lost his pop sensibility. 'Place in the Sun' highlights McComb's talent for writing memorable melodies, and the importance he placed on (re)arranging his songs. The Triffids, as a collective, deserve credit for forging a style that was beguiling whether they were playing a pop song like 'Goodbye Little Boy' or accompanying epic, dramatic monologues like 'Stolen Property' or 'Save What You Can'.

'Red Pony' (1983): The visionary

The opening track from The Triffids first full-length album, 'Red Pony' throws the gauntlet down to the band's peers. It gallops out of the blocks, conveying a complex mix of youthful passion, lust and confusion. Composed around an insistent bass line, the song reveals McComb's sense of grandeur through its sweeping string arrangement. It's a long way from the guitar and synth-based music of the era. Although I'd heard the track played live many times, the sonic force of this recording made me stop to catch my breath. The song shifts between 6/8 and 3/4 time, creating a fluid and lilting feel. This temporal alternation adds a sense of unease as it moves between moments of stability and disorientation.

Although the lyrics are sparse, comprising a single verse repeated with minor alterations, the song evokes a compelling narrative. Bleddyn Butcher praises the writing, noting that the line:

> 'Sand in your eye/Sun upon your back' is not just a neat way of describing a girl asleep on the beach. It also introduces the idea of injury – 'sand in your eye', which 'black' and 'blind' then build upon – and evokes the shifting landscape of a dream. Singer and pony are one, united by blindness, blinded by love's glorious light.
>
> (2011, 121)

'Red Pony' is a key song in McComb's repertoire, signifying the scope of his lyrical and sonic ambition and his ability to give voice to complex emotions. McComb noted, 'The purpose of *Red Pony* was to make the lyrics minimal and abstract, so there was no more rational a message in the words than there was in the music' (1990).

'Jesus Calling' (1984): The secular pilgrim

It is hard to ignore McComb's interest in religion. McComb once declared, 'I have no religious persuasion at all but there is such a pool of great images [in religion] which can be pulled into popular culture' (quoted in Reid, 2023). Critics often draw attention to religious symbols and ideas in his work (McGowan, 2009; Stratton, 2009). McComb's interest in religion is most apparent on his solo album, *Love of Will* (1994), but 'Jesus Calling', the opening track on the *Raining Pleasure* mini-LP (The Triffids 1984), provides me with an opportunity to explore how McComb's dedication to his art was akin to a religious calling.

McComb lived for his craft. Several friends and bandmates, some of whom contribute to *Truckload of Sky*, testify to McComb's obsession with songwriting. Graham Lee recalls he had met no one who took songwriting as seriously as David. Phil Kakulas concurs and notes that David would do anything to create the next song (*Love in Bright Landscapes*, 2020). It would not be hyperbolic to argue that David McComb was following a vocation in the religious sense of the word. McComb's parents brought him up as a Presbyterian. He attended church regularly and, won a prize for divinity when he was a student at Christ Church Grammar School, yet he never professed to be especially religious. Andrew McGowan (2009), a school friend who played in an early incarnation of The Triffids, has written an eloquent essay on McComb's use of Christian imagery and concepts in his songs. McGowan, an Anglican Minister, and theologian, suggests that McComb's use of religious imagery had more to do with his reading of American Southern Gothic literature than any deep commitment to a supernatural deity. In 1985, McComb told RAM magazine about his obsession with Flannery O'Connor's writing: 'I've read everything of hers, and she's been much more important to me than any musical influence for the past year and a half' (Ryan 1985). McComb frequently incorporated religious imagery and symbols into his songs, although he often expressed his interest in spirituality within a Nietzschean framework: if God is dead, what fills the void left by the absence of God in our culture?

I use the term 'vocation' in its religious sense to show that McComb saw writing and songwriting as being something akin to a religious calling. The word 'vocation' in its religious sense refers to an individual's sense of being singled out by God to follow a religious path; this requires deep faith and significant sacrifice. Writing, if one is as serious about the craft as McComb was, requires faith in one's abilities and entails a significant personal cost. In 'Jesus Calling', the narrator is confronted with a choice amidst competing demands. Prioritizing activities such as scratching an itch, making a match and catching a fish, the 'I' neglects his relationship with his lover. The narrator sings: 'I'm going to have to call this whole thing off now/I'm going to have to nip it in the bud/I have Jesus/I have Jesus calling me.' Of course, we can read the lyrics literally as being about having a telephone conversation with the man who stilled the waters (Butcher, 2011, 153) but it also, I think, dramatizes the conflict between having any kind of 'calling' that interferes with the demands of one's personal life.[3] It is this latter struggle that made McComb's personal life so difficult.

'Field of Glass' (1985): The actor

Bands, as Clinton Walker points out, exist as performers on stage and as recording artists (2021, 307). I attended my first

---

[3]   The conceit of talking to Jesus on the telephone occurs in Mississippi Fred McDowell's 'Jesus Is on the Mainline', which Ry Cooder covered on *Paradise and Lunch* (1974). McComb may have heard Jimmy Little's 1963 record 'Royal Telephone' which uses the same trope.

Triffids gig in 1982 and became an instant convert. However, I thought, and still believe, that the band's recordings on vinyl represent them best. McComb's penchant for epic atmospheric productions required a plethora of guest musicians to paint a complex sonic picture that required various overdubs and studio effects. It was not practical or economical for the band to reproduce the sound of their records live – not that The Triffids were not a great live band. They could mix it with the best bands of the era on stage and won an award for being WA's best live band in 1985. That said, 'Field of Glass' is one of the few Triffids songs that I thought worked better live than on vinyl. In 1983, McComb told *RAM*, 'We'd rather be known for our records than our live performances … potentially we're better on record' (cited in Butcher, 2011, 142). By 1984, though, The Triffids' live act had become harder, more theatrical. I first saw them in 1982. By this time, the band no longer lived in Perth but returned periodically, mostly during the holiday season towards the end of the year.

I saw The Triffids as often as I could, sometimes two or three nights a week. On one occasion, I witnessed them twice in a single night – the second performance that evening was memorable because of a fight between two drunken louts. I recall McComb heroically restoring order by jumping off the stage and separating the principal aggressors.

On stage, McComb could be droll and genial, but was not averse to admonishing the sometimes-complacent crowd for requesting familiar songs, and cover versions of other people's hits (which the band appeared to enjoy playing). There were always one or two die-hard fans that felt the need to share their intimate knowledge of the band's earliest songs by rowdily requesting 'Butterfly' or, more often, 'Farmers Never Visit Nightclubs' (a song I will revisit in the next chapter). Depending on his mood, McComb would acquiesce or dismiss these calls from the crowd.

Friendly hecklers notwithstanding, the band was committed to their music; their shows comprised furious sermons from the pulpit, atmospheric missives from a lonely place, and twee ditties delivered with just the right degree of irony. For all the dark and brooding songs in McComb's canon, the band had a sense of humour, and seemed to relish playing cheesy Vegas-era Elvis covers alongside incendiary garage band classics like '96 Tears' and 'No Fun'. Their version of the theme from *Gilligan's Island* underscores their eclecticism and capacity for comedy.

By the time 'Field of Glass' was part of the band's live repertoire, McComb had become a more compelling performer, and continued to grow in confidence throughout the rest of The Triffids' career, commanding the stage, adopting a range of personas to suit the mood of his songs: the fiery backwoods preacher, the fearsome moralist, the spurned lover, the soulful crooner, the sensitive poet, the desperate outlaw and the respectful acolyte (when he covered the songs of his heroes). Butcher believes McComb had written in character from quite an early point in his career (2011, 147). However, his live performances of songs like 'Field of Glass' show that he'd developed a strong dramatic technique.

The song itself is a mash-up of sorts. It incorporates 'Pleasure Slide', which appears on a live-to-air recording made by Melbourne radio station 3PBS in April 1984. The completed song entered the band's repertoire a few months later in all its ferocious glory (a live recording is available on the *Come Ride With Me … Wide Open Road* Box Set). I hear 'Field of Glass' as a garage band thrash, despite its twists and turns. Butcher describes it as 'a piece of theatrical voodoo, a lurid mixture of gnomic boasting and paranoid fantasy' (2011, 216). The twin guitar attack of the McComb brothers on this song always impressed me with its ferocity, which I don't believe the vinyl recording possesses.

I couldn't make sense of the song's lyrics when I first heard the band perform this monumental homage to lust and rage, but the band's sonic assault conveyed the gist of the mood. Sometimes, the grain of the singer's voice says more than the literal meaning of the lyrics. For the record, the song's narrator implores his coy mistress to abandon caution and give the middle finger to parental authority. The narrator wants to fuck: 'Come ride with me', he roars. However, the ironic backing vocals undercut the bluesy boast by echoing lines like 'I eat razors, too' – McComb's 'posse' punctuates his persona's bluesy macho bluster – Muddy Waters, Howling Wolf and Bo Diddly can rest easy.

'The Seabirds' (1986): The 'Moodist'

This track appears on The Triffids' masterpiece, *Born Sandy Devotional* (*BSD*). Independently financed and recorded in the UK, the record represents a milestone in the band's development. Unlike the band's debut, McComb conceived *BSD* as a set of thematically connected songs about unrequited love. Each tune depicts a character in a state of feverish, often hysterical despair. The album is notable for its atmospheric, moody production, which uses a distinctive aural palette. Pedal steel, lap steel, vibraphone and strings expand and complement the usual blend of guitars, keyboards and drums. Unnerving glissandos, orchestral percussion and spooky melodic motifs characterize the sound of *BSD*. McComb's lyrics frequently use landscape features as both literal settings and metaphors for unsettling states of being. The album evokes a gothic mood, suffused with mystery, morbidity and gloom. If there is any substance to the claim that The Triffids are a quintessentially Australian band, it might be because McComb's references to the Australian landscape connect him to the tradition of Australian gothic literature. These narratives often represent the outback as a haunted space, populated by malevolent forces. Indeed, Roslynn Haynes contends that the 'very emptiness of the desert led the explorers to people it with ghosts' (1999, 82).

'The Seabirds' marries a set of striking natural images (sand, sea, reef, sky, birds) to tell a concise story about a bereft, 'washed-up', lovelorn figure. Like so many songs on *Born Sandy Devotional*, 'The Seabirds' is cinematic. The first verse is a wide establishing shot, pregnant with menace. The second uses a tighter framing to expose details about the isolated lover's state of mind. He is swimming to his doom without regard for his welfare since he's already dead inside.

It begins without musical preamble: the singer comes in with the music almost immediately, assumes an omniscient third-person point of view and narrates the story of a broken man on the brink of emotional collapse. No foreign pair of sunglasses can shield him from the white light of truth and the ominous sound of gulls screeching overhead, announcing or echoing the disconsolate figure's sense of impending ruin.[4] Establishing a vague geographical location, the coastal imagery, which will recur throughout the album, leaves room

---

[4]   There is a sense in which the 'foreign' sunglasses cannot
      protect its owner (presumably a white colonial settler) from the
      oppressively bright Australian light. This reinforces the idea that
      the Australian landscape functions as a metaphor for alienation in
      the song (and throughout *Born Sandy Devotional*).

for interpretation, as the seabirds could be circling any coastal region. The predatory birds circling and swarming around the sky serve as powerful metaphors, offering an aerial view of the helpless protagonist as they viciously attack their prey, transforming the water into a crimson hue and casting an eerie glow upon the sky – creating a menacing backdrop for the unfolding drama. Without emotion, the seabirds hunt their victims as creatures of instinct.

The lonely figure takes himself away from all human company and consolation, swimming to the edge of the reef, and the brink of sanity. His loneliness is of such magnitude that his senses fail him. He can't feel physical pain – the sting of the saltwater on serrated flesh cannot divert him from his loneliness, nor can he hear those voices that may talk him out of slipping over the edge ('little boy, it doesn't have to end this way').

The third verse cuts to a flashback that reveals the source of the man's hurt. He's separated from his lover; he's announced their 'trial separation' but suspects that the break is permanent. His attempts to find solace in alcohol and casual sex are futile. Nature once again provides ominous imagery to heighten the emotional tone of the song. This time the rain falls hard on the motel roof, as the temporary partner of McComb's character asks: 'Are you drinking to get maudlin or drinking to get numb?' Is he drinking to conjure sentiment, or drinking to numb the loss he's suffered? Of course, we don't get an answer, for the question can't be settled. He could be trying to do both. Is it better to feel nothing, or feel too much when someone shatters your heart? Either way, our hapless protagonist is inconsolable.

The final verse cuts back to the beach where the wounded man exhorts the malevolent birds to put him out of his misery, for death is the only panacea for his kind of pain. The birds, creatures capable of striking prey with great precision, refuse to go near such a damaged soul – they leave him to scream at an indifferent sky: 'where were you, where were you?' He remains a pathetic figure, stranded in an ominous landscape, hankering after a death the seabirds refuse to deliver.

McComb's landscapes are also, I believe, 'eerie' in Fisher's sense of the word, which denotes a hauntological affect. Fisher distinguishes between two related affects produced by art: the 'weird' and the 'eerie'. He calls something 'weird' if it does not fit in the world of a particular narrative. He contrasts the frightening with the unsettling weird. He makes his point by comparing a vampire with a black hole. While vampires might be frightening, they are made from familiar elements – recognizable parts of our world and human traits, though twisted into something menacing. More importantly, we have a wealth of myths and stories that help us understand these creatures when we encounter them in fiction. A black hole, however, is a different beast. It is beyond comprehension, as are the mind-bending effects it has, like warping the flow of time. Dark matter and dark energy fall into the same category – despite their apparent existence, it's hard to wrap our minds around the idea that invisible forms of matter and energy are shaping the very fabric of our visible universe.

The 'eerie' is produced in space: landscapes, ruined cityscapes, dilapidated houses and so on. The eerie is a kind of environmental affect most readily apprehended in places totally or partially devoid of humans (Fisher 2016, 11). While the weird is defined by an incongruous presence, the eerie is defined by an unsettling absence, which generates the following questions:

What happened to produce these ruins, this disappearance? What kind of entity was involved? What kind of thing was it that emitted such an eerie cry? As we can see from these examples, the eerie is fundamentally tied up with questions of agency. What kind of agent is acting here? Is there an agent at all?

(2016, 11)

The songs on *Born Sandy Devotional* often evoke the eerie atmosphere of diverse geographical locations, including a perilous reef, a beach, an estuary, a solitary stretch of dark road, a bridge and a vast, empty sky above a desert wilderness. McComb's lyrics, and the band's atmospheric music, imbue these references to the natural environment (land, sky, beach, reef, desert) with a sense of malevolent agency.

The early films of Peter Weir, especially *Picnic at Hanging Rock* (1975) and *The Last Wave* (1977), provide antipodean examples of the eerie. For example, the incessant wind and rain in *The Last Wave* appear to seek human victims. In an early scene, these forces of nature smash the windows in a remote classroom, resulting in a student getting injured and instilling fear in his classmates. Weir's next film provides a better example of the eerie. *Picnic at Hanging Rock*, a film Fisher cites in his book, is about the mysterious disappearance of three schoolgirls and a teacher during a trip to Hanging Rock, a geological formation in central Victoria, approximately ninety minutes from Melbourne. The absence of any explanation for their disappearance – whether natural, supernatural or human-caused – creates an eerie atmosphere.

This mirrors Fisher's idea of the eerie as rooted in the unsettling absence of something that should be there (in this case, the girls and teacher). The film depicts Hanging Rock itself as a place that is both beautiful and ominous. Through its ancient, enigmatic presence, the rock formation becomes a character, embodying the eerie. Echoing Fisher's notion of the eerie as a place where the boundaries between the natural and the supernatural blur, the rock possesses an agency that disrupts the normal course of events. In these films, Weir gives the Australian landscape a mysterious and malevolent agency in a way that resonates with McComb's treatment of outback settings.

'Suntrapper' (1986): The surrealist

'Suntrapper' appears on *In the Pines*, an album recorded in a woolshed on the McComb family's property in Ravensthorpe, a town 541 km south-east of Perth and 40 km inland from the south coast of Western Australia. On one level, the record sounds like the sonic antithesis of *Born Sandy Devotional*, yet it is every bit as atmospheric as its more celebrated predecessor. Recorded on a hired eight-track machine, the album is low-fi, especially in contrast to the lush studio sounds on *Born Sandy Devotional*. *In the Pines*, though, is also a kind of landscape album in a different sense. The rural environment seeps into the recording. It's possible to hear the room tone as a sonic feature of the record; it's almost an instrument. The album has a folky quality courtesy of the liberal use of acoustic guitars, violin and mandolin. The band also stomps on floorboards and whacks a water tank with a broom. Bruce Callaway, the recording engineer and album's co-producer, recalled:

> David very clearly wanted the woolshed atmosphere to be kept. A room microphone was recorded on nearly all the tracks and he wanted this to be used. It was meant to be rough and full of life. He wanted as much of the noises, sounds and chatter in between the takes to be included.
>
> (2006)

Blending surreal and symbolic imagery, the lyrics of 'Suntrapper' tell a mysterious and haunting story. The song's narrator recounts a fateful night when something extraordinary and unsettling happens in his small, humble town (Perth? Ravensthorpe? Jerdacuttup?). Without warning, the mysterious figure or force known as the 'Suntrapper' takes the narrator's sister away. The song presents this event as deeply traumatic, and it leaves the narrator grappling with a profound sense of loss and confusion.

The lyrics combine a variety of striking, almost apocalyptic visuals – like tall glass buildings, the splitting open of the ground, falling trees, and jet engines ripping apart a house – with a sense of personal sorrow. The Suntrapper represents the powerful, mysterious force that steals the narrator's sister, leaving behind unresolved pain and unanswered questions. What kind of thing is a Suntrapper? A monster? A malevolent spirit? A UFO? Why did his sister lay her body down? Where has she gone? Where is the narrator going? What kind of fearsome power does the mysterious entity possess? By dramatizing something otherworldly intruding into the everyday lives of ordinary people, the song resonates with Fisher's account of the weird (the Suntrapper is an incongruous presence).[5]

'Jerdacuttup Man' (1987): The autobiographer

This song appears on *Calenture*, the band's major label debut. After almost a decade of toil, The Triffids were on the verge of

---

[5]   Fisher's formulation of the Weird resonates with surrealism's obsession with incongruous objects (the meeting of a sewing machine and an umbrella on an operating table). The Eerie, on the other hand, is more closely related to the Gothic.

mainstream success, having signed a deal with Island Records. Critics acclaimed the album at the time of its release in 1987 (Butcher, 2011, 380–1). Unfortunately, critical praise did not translate into large sales. Today, people seem to either love or hate the album. It is included in the book, *1001 Albums You Must Hear before You Die*, which notes that McComb's 'poetry (for it surely is) fuels songs that burn with loss and longing' (2021, 579). A cursory glance at the comments written by the book's readers, available on the book's website, shows many people don't like the record's glossy 1980s production pointing to the lush reverb effects and the drum sound.

Most of the songs on the record are about the deleterious effects of McComb's vocation. According to the album's sleeve notes 'calenture' is a 'tropical fever or delirium suffered by sailors after long periods away from land, who imagine the seas to be green fields and desire to leap into them' (1987). By the time the album was recorded, The Triffids had been away from their homes and loved ones for long stretches of time, which explains why McComb identified with this nautical malady:

> I was fed up with not living anywhere. Everyone in the group was in a stable relationship except me and Graham Lee. I remember one time on a ferry, crossing the Icelandic Sea or something like that, and Graham just said to me, oh, if this keeps up I'm going to bloody die. I took him at his word.
>
> (Quoted in Walker, 2021, 365)

While acknowledging that being signed to a major international record label represented the apex of his career, McComb confessed to Clinton Walker that he'd been depressed since completing the record: 'I mean, how much longer do you go on leaving girlfriends behind in Australia?' (2021, 303). McComb's songs often drew on his personal life. Graham Lee remarked that 'if his relationships hadn't struggled, we might not have gotten some of those songs' (Personal Interview, 2024). While I don't believe we can wholly attribute the quality of McComb's songs to his personal life, there is little doubt that there is an autobiographical dimension to a lot of his work.

Calenture, like *Born Sandy Devotional* before it and *The Black Swan* after it, is a concept album of sorts. McComb's lyrics are marked by ambiguities and mysteries that invite a wide range of readings, but it isn't hard to see how McComb might have identified himself with the lonesome climbing figure who slips and loses grips while climbing a mountain in the album's opening track, 'Bury Me Deep in Love'. McComb's regular use of religious imagery makes connections between his vocation as a songwriter and the idea of a religious calling. Put differently, art, for him, is religion, songs provide solace in the face of existential despair and can function as a source of salvation. McComb addresses this theme in 'Make Believe We're Not Here in Hell' on *Truckload of Sky*.

He addresses the pitfalls of his demanding vocation, however, in other registers, too. The song 'Jerdacuttup Man', for example, sees McComb identifying with a mummified body in the British Museum. He gives voice to the dead figure, frozen in time, in a dramatic monologue that disturbs the boundary between singer and character. Jerdacuttup is a small town in the southwest of Western Australia, a region that has personal significance for McComb, whose family owned a farm in that area of the state (Butcher, 2011, 18).[6] He notes that the hapless

---

[6]   This rural property played an important role in McComb's life. As previously mentioned, The Triffids recorded *In the Pines* on the family farm, but the location appears to have been a formative influence on McComb's literary sensibility.

figure, preserved in peat, and who 'had no luck in business and no luck in love', met his untimely demise in his prime. In the last verse of the song, the narrator issues a desperate plea: 'won't you please take me home'. This longing for home is the autobiographical core of this 'weird' song, which expresses a sentiment that McComb returns to on *Truckload of Sky's* 'So Good to be Home'.

'New Years Greetings' (1989): The poet

This song highlights McComb's literary sensibility. It's another epic dramatic monologue (in the same vein as tracks like 'Stolen Property' and 'Save What You Can' and, as we shall see in my commentary on *Truckload of Sky*, 'This Whole World's About to Slide'). 'New Years Greetings' appears on *The Black Swan*, The Triffids' final album. This is the group's most eclectic work, intended, deliberately, to be like The Beatles' *White Album* (released as *The Beatles* in 1968) in terms of its references to different musical styles the record is suffused with elements drawn from hip-hop, electronica, rock, jazz, soul and even opera.

Unfortunately, Island Records released a single disc version of *The Black Swan*, so the band did not realize their expansive vision for the recording until Domino (and Liberation Blue in Australia) reissued it as a double album in 2007. While some critics found the work confusing and directionless, I've always been a fan of McComb's eclecticism, which freely engages in a dialogue with spectral voices from several musical traditions.

'New Years Greeting' begins with McComb and a female backing singer scatting the song's main melodic motif (strings and electric guitar repeat this motif at various points in the song). This sets a wistful, reflective mood for the monologue that unfolds. We learn the narrator has retreated to 'Stony Ridge', where he lives with 'a good black dog'.[7] He potters around, living on welfare. He's got no job, no commitments. He can leave his bed unmade. He whistles along with the tunes he hears on AM radio. He declares he doesn't want to be bothered by the outside world, he doesn't 'Need no Eyewitness News/No 7-Eleven/No Southern Fried Chicken/No man from Prudential'.

The details of his laid-back routine suggest that he's doing fine. He's free from all responsibilities, or so it seems. Butcher points out that the song 'exploits the potential of drip feeding' (2011, 402). The slow release of detail culminates in a striking revelation. Like so many of McComb's characters, the ghost of a lost lover haunts the narrator of 'New Years Greetings'. Here, on Stony Ridge, things get spooky when the sun goes down. The wind that whistles through the landscape 'shudders to a halt' and the washed-out main roads leave the narrator stranded, bereft, contemplating the absence of his former love ('the gaping lack of you and me') which is symbolized by the all-encompassing blackness that stretches 'as far as the eye can see'. Try as he might, the narrator just can't let things go. He knows his paramour has taken up with another – she's riding 'a

---

[7]   The black dog is often used as a symbol for depression, which makes the phrase 'good black dog' a little odd until the narrator reveals that he doesn't need a phone because his canine companion 'can smell bad weather coming in his old dog bones'. These lyrics suggest that the narrator's dog may not be an actual animal, but a kind of sixth sense. Either way, the song, like the Les Murray poem that inspired it, 'The Widower In The Country' (Murray 1989), is about a depressive mood that comes from the experience of loss and loneliness.

new horse in the sun' (another 'red pony', no doubt). What can a poor boy do? The narrator sends New Year's greetings, but still wants his lover back despite all that has passed between them.

McComb wrote his own account of the song's origins in *Juke* in 1990:

> This was initially a short story but was persuaded to become a song. The idea of a middle-aged farmer narrating a pop song was intensely appealing to me, as was the opportunity to let him rant against as [sic] few of his most despised multi-national corporate products (who says The Triffids aren't political?), itemise his daily routine, and berate the smugness of Sydneysiders.
>
> Most of the (West Australia) rural detail is extremely real to me, but the idea owes a massive debt to Les Murray's poem 'The Widower In The Country', which can be found in his *Vernacular Republic* anthology. Also, less obviously, to an absolutely fantastic poem called 'New Year Letter' which the great Russian poet Marina Tsvetaeva wrote upon hearing of Rilke's death in 1927. Both this poem and Joseph Brodsky's related essay are guaranteed to change lives.

The memory of the narrator's lost love is not the only ghost that haunts the song. As mentioned earlier in this chapter, the logic of hauntology unsettles the idea that texts are self-sufficient, and McComb's poetic phantoms manifest in this compelling track. Butcher points out that McComb used Marina Tsvetaeva's poem, 'New Year Letter' (2009), as an inspiration for his song. Tsvetaeva conducted a passionate epistolary relationship with the German poet Rainer Maria Rilke, another of McComb's literary heroes. The two writers never met. Rilke received six letters from the Russian, who had written nine letters and a postcard to him (Tavis, 1993, 494). Upon learning of his death, Tsvetaeva expressed their immaterial passion in her elegy to Rilke. The poem addresses a ghost.

'The Message' (1991): The alchemist

As previously discussed, McComb had an eclectic taste in music. This is clear in his choice of cover songs, which, in the late 1980s and early 1990s, included tracks from the likes of Madonna, Prince and The Pet Shop Boys. He listened attentively to Top 40 music on the radio. He was also a fan of hip-hop, although he resisted the temptation to attempt 'white boy' rap, though, that said, 'Falling over You' from *The Black Swan* comes close. Chris Coughran reminds us that McComb saw rap and hip-hop artists as contemporary poets (2009, 270–1). In an interview with Swedish radio, McComb praised LL Cool J, comparing him to Charles Dickens for 'relishing in words' (1991). McComb's comments about 'Going Back to Cali' convey his love of language and wordplay. He confessed that he's 'willing to be bewitched' by beautiful words regardless of subject or moral considerations. McComb was fond of LL Cool J's *Walking with a Panther* (1989), and I suspect Rick Rubin's 'radio-friendly' production impressed him as much as the rapper's sly wordplay. The lyrics of 'One Shot of Love' are in the same general wheelhouse as McComb's lyrics on 'The Message', a single he released with Adam Peters in 1991.[8]

---

[8]   Based in the UK after The Triffids' demise, McComb and Peters collaborated on a few singles as McComb tried to find a new direction in the early 1990s.

Programmed drums, synthesizers and female backing vocals are used in the track, along with stabs of electric guitar and a solid dose of sub-bass thump. The Triffids experimented with drum machines and various bits of modern technology from about 1986 (their most acclaimed song, 'Wide Open Road', uses a drum machine), but 'The Message' sees McComb embrace a dance/techno sound with gusto.

'The Message' is on my McComb mixtape because it represents his penchant for musical adventure with scant regard for what people thought he should be doing. He was always searching for unfamiliar sounds and new ways to present his lyrics. 'The Message' is a song about the singer's search for a soul mate: 'I have a name inside my head/I was given it at birth/All I have to do is find you/Before I leave this earth.' Like Cool J, the character in this song has 'one shot' to find his love, but the lyrics also resonate with Aristophanes' speech in Plato's *Symposium*, which McComb encountered in one of Elizabeth Jolly's creative writing classes at WAIT (Butcher, 2011, 42).[9] The satirical playwright regales the assembly of Athenian luminaries with a story about how we were all once creatures with four arms and two legs until Zeus cut humans in half, condemning them to spend their lives looking for their other half. This ludicrous myth is possibly the source for the song's lyrics.

---

[9] Celebrated novelist, Elizabeth Jolly (1923–2007) had yet to make her mark as a writer when she taught McComb in the early 1980s. Jolly's comments on McComb's assignments suggest she was impressed by his writing. Butcher quotes extracts from Jolly's feedback on some of McComb's work: 'I've given this the highest possible mark … because, on reflection, there's an enormous amount of creativity & control (which in your case is creativity) in the main work' (quoted in Butcher, 2011, 44).

'I Want to Conquer You' (1994, 2007, 2009): The writer

This song is from *Love of Will*, but it's Melanie Oxley's cover version I'd include on my mixtape. McComb's songs, by his own admission, were personal, often inspired by traumatic incidents in his emotional life. And while he performed his own material brilliantly, sometimes cover versions by other artists do more to highlight his strengths as a songwriter. Indeed, *Truckload of Sky* shows that McComb's songs stand on their own given the right singer. As an avid Triffids fan, I'd thought no one could sing McComb's songs better than he did. Then I heard Melanie Oxley and Chris Abrahams perform 'Embedded' and 'I Want to Conquer You' at the Sydney Festival in 2007 as part of the 'A Secret in the Shape of a Song' concert. The latter song, which I found revelatory, begins with stripped back instrumentation (vocal and piano) before building in intensity as the band kick in. If I did not realize it before, Oxley proved that McComb's songs have a life of their own. In fact, familiarity with McComb's autobiographical inspirations for his songs can occlude their complexity.

If you've ever been emotionally drained by an intimate, all-night conversation with a lover, this song will resonate with you. Dawn is breaking, you've made your case, there's nothing left to say except 'I want to conquer you'. This is an ambiguous phrase. What might it mean? I want to fuck you? I want to win you over, before 'love wanes' and time's winged chariot sends us both to the grave? I want to overpower you with love?

Oxley stamps a whispery authority over these lyrics, shifting the song's mood through her dramatic inflections and pauses. Oxley, during the performance, seems to be in a trance; eyes closed tightly, she sways as the song picks up pace and moves into its bridge. It's as though she's addressing a lover through the song. Her performance is filled with an aching longing, a stark intimacy. I think Oxley does a better job of selling the song's emotional complexities than McComb. Unfortunately, 'I Want to Conquer You' is not available on CD or vinyl, but it's accessible on YouTube. Angie Hart, a contributor to *Truckload of Sky*, also captures the song's intimate qualities in her version of the song, which is available on her album, *Eat My Shadow* (2009). Both women uncover emotional nuances through their quite different approaches. Having a woman sing the song gives it a different emotional resonance.

In a publicity blurb for Mushroom Records, McComb described the composition as 'a love song about Germany's annexation of Poland, the soviet invasion of Czechoslovakia, Hungary etc etc (Kuwait, Bosnia … fill in your own love story)' (1995). Clearly, the man had a droll sense of humour, which, I suspect, the record company publicists may not have appreciated.

'By Your Hand' (1996): The mentor

In 1988, David formed a 'holiday' band called The Bottomless Schooners of Old with a few friends, including Rob Snarski and Phil Kakulas. This casual outfit, based in Perth, morphed into The Blackeyed Susans the following year. While McComb wrote and sang a substantial number of songs on the first few albums released by this group, Rob Snarski was the lead singer. McComb left the Blackeyed Susans in 1993 to focus on his solo career. He formed another band, The Red Ponies, to promote the *Love of Will* album.

McComb had long admired Snarski's smooth vocals and became his friend, mentor and collaborator. Snarski refers to his friendship with McComb in his memoir, *You're Not Rob Snarski, Crumbs from the Cake* (2017).

> David McComb was forever encouraging me to put myself in the spotlight, to get out there and sing. At times random, unexpected moments. There were instances where he was frustrated, drained by my lack of confidence, my inability to deliver a lyric, culminating in some delicate and brutal home truths in the studio. 'Sing The Song!'
>
> (2017, 85)

'By Your Hand' is a McComb/Snarski co-write, which appears on The Blackeyed Susans' *Mouth to Mouth* (1996) album. I've included the song on my McComb mixtape to underscore his collaborative spirit and the value he placed on the affective qualities of singing. Snarski told Kristen Krauth that McComb

> wasn't one to just sing the song. You had to tell the tale within the song. You had to deliver the words. It's very important. He really stretched my singing capabilities. I was really reticent as a singer. I was quite a shy person and Dave essentially pushed me in front of the microphone and encouraged me to do. It wasn't about melodic rhythms or being in pitch. Being in tune mattered as much as the genuine delivery of the lyric to draw you in.
>
> (Almost a Mirror Podcast, 2022)

Snarski nails the song's lyric, which is about surrendering oneself to those forces that are beyond our control. The imagery of seeds blown by the wind symbolizes a lack of control over one's destiny. The narrator might be addressing a lover, or a higher power such as God or fate. Either way, Snarski takes McComb's advice and expertly conveys the idea that it's possible to find solace in submission.

'The Good Life Never Ends' (1998): The mortal

McComb recorded this song with his last band, costar.[10] The song is a monologue about the vicissitudes of fortune. The narrator is a lonely wanderer reflecting on his life, his friends and lovers. The song's ironic title, which repeats throughout the composition, alludes to broken dreams, failed ambitions. As we know, McComb's quest did not end in commercial success, and he had every reason to feel depressed about his relative lack of acclaim in the 1990s. His only solo album did not emerge until 1994 and by that time he was too unwell to promote it, although he formed a band, which included luminaries like Jim White and Warren Ellis, both of The Dirty Three, for that purpose. In what was possibly his last radio interview, McComb modestly rejects the suggestion that he had become a bona fide legend.

McComb sounds weary and impaired on the live-to-air costar version of the song, which makes it even more poignant. This wistful track must have been a contender for *Truckload*

---

[10] Julian Wu recorded six costar songs, which, at the time of writing, remain unreleased. He recorded 'The Good Life Never Ends' as part of this project. Costar also performed the song on a live-to-air broadcast, which was recorded at The Esplanade Hotel, St. Kilda in August 1998.

of Sky (hopefully it will appear on a subsequent volume of McComb's lost songs). It's on my mixtape for its emotional gravitas, which shows McComb's steely determination to keep chasing the muse under dire circumstances. McComb never lost his vocation. His artistic vision remained strong and true until the end.

The final track on this first mixtape chapter, however, is not McComb's version of the song. Instead, I've chosen Rob Snarski's performance of 'The Good Life Never Ends', which appears on the *Raining Pleasure* DVD (recorded at the Metro Theatre as part of the Sydney Arts Festival in 2008). A grief-stricken Snarski struggles to get past the first few lines. He turns his back on the hushed audience, while the band look on with expressions of concern and empathy for their distraught friend. Handsome Steve Miller, the concert MC, consoles Snarski and suggests that the band strike up a different song. Snarski eases Miller aside, steps up to the microphone and, with eyes still moist from his tears, delivers a powerful rendition of this perturbing song. The performance conveys the depth of Snarski's love for his late friend and mentor. He composes himself, and *sings* the *song*.

2   A Perth mixtape

Critics and scholars often write about The Triffids' connection to the city of Perth and the landscape of Western Australia. Indeed, a focus on place, locality and Australian mythology permeates several key books and articles about McComb's songs (Brabazon, 2005; Cull, 2005; Stratton, 2007; Stratton and Trainer, 2016). These writings often probe The Triffids' reputation as a quintessentially Australian band. McComb's lyrics often use the vast, barren spaces of outback Australia locations as literal settings or as metaphors for various emotional states. Perth's distance from Australia's other major population centres also plays an important role in many of McComb's songs. Perth is the only major city on Australia's west coast and it's about 2,694 km from Adelaide, its nearest urban neighbour. Sydney and Melbourne, Australia's biggest cities, lie further east. After Honolulu, Perth is the world's most isolated city. Many Perthites are suspicious of the 'eastern states', whose inhabitants often dismiss the West Australian capital as a dull cultural backwater (Newman, 2016; Stratton and Trainer, 2016).

Perth's population in the 1980s was just under a million people. While this number may give some people the impression that Perth is more of a small town than bona fide city, it's important to remember, with Brabazon (2005), that the history of pop music is littered with examples of relatively small urban centres giving birth to vital and influential music scenes: Liverpool (Merseybeat), Detroit (Motown; proto punk) and Seattle (Grunge) to name a few obvious examples (although McComb's major influences came from New York). Brabazon argues:

There are two elements that frame distinctiveness for Perth music. Extreme isolation generates insularity, protectiveness and self-satisfaction. Interweaving with this inwardness is a huge immigrant population that creates an associative web between cities, thereby encouraging extreme outwardness and interconnectedness.

(2005, 2)

This insularity was compounded by the fact that major touring acts opted out of visiting Perth. This might account for the city's obsession with cover bands.

In this chapter, I will compile and annotate another mixtape. This one will use songs McComb wrote about Perth and Australia as prompts to sketch a picture of his cultural context focusing particularly on The Triffids place in the Australian music scene during the 1980s. Before hitting the play button on our virtual cassette deck, it's worth pointing out that McComb held a variety of contrasting views about Perth. David Nichols cites an interview from the early 1980s in which McComb stated that living in Perth was 'a bit like being in an incubator, being bottled somewhere', although he also claimed that the inhabitants of his hometown 'have a bit of spirit and personality' (2009, 81). In 1983, he told Clinton Walker the band 'felt more suffocated in Melbourne than we ever had in Perth. In Perth I never felt, I never felt like busting out of it, I really quite liked living there. [But] it's just not practical' (Walker, 2023, 161). In a 1993 promotional interview for his solo album, *Love of Will*, McComb was asked about his memories of the Perth music scene: 'We didn't think it was a lively music scene at the time, but looking back, it was. I was a teenager seeing lots of punk bands. Punk was a big thing for me at around 15 and 16' (1993).

In private, though, he could be scornful about his birthplace. Butcher quotes an extract from a private letter: 'I fear I turn up unwelcome in Perth – it has become a foreign, horrifying place to me – but I fear my sorrow with Perth is a feeling too unexplainable to ever fall upon receptive ears. You must think I'm crazy!' (quoted in Butcher, 2011, 272).

The local music press never paid too much attention to The Triffids even during the latter half of the eighties when they had achieved more recognition in Europe than most of their big-name counterparts in Australia. Bands such as Midnight Oil, Mondo Rock, Australian Crawl and Cold Chisel may have dominated the Australian charts but made negligible impact overseas. Certainly, the West Australian press gave more attention to bands such as V-Capri and Boys, groups that started out as cover bands before attempting to find success in the 'eastern states' with their original material. McComb's antipathy towards Perth might have had something to do with this lack of recognition.

Perth's major music magazine of the time, *X-Press*, was especially obsessed with the now almost forgotten V-Capri, a cover band that pulled enormous crowds from the mid-1980s. Mushroom Records signed the group, who had attempted to morph into an original power pop band. They released an album, *In My World*, in the same year The Triffids released *Born Sandy Devotional* (1986). McComb and The Triffids had good cause to feel slighted by the failure of local journalists to recognize the band's achievements. This may explain why McComb's later songs about Perth are more critical of the city's insular cultural tendencies. The following annotations highlight the extent to which McComb used his songwriting to record his thoughts and feelings about his cultural environment, his place in the sun.

'Martyrs' (1978)

> It gets a little boring, but that doesn't matter
> Because we're martyrs, martyrs of Perth punk

In 1977, *Countdown* was the biggest, and most influential, popular music show on Australian television. Hosted by Ian 'Molly' Meldrum, *Countdown* played a mixture of video clips, sourced from Europe and the United States and lip-synched studio performances by local acts. Molly's tastes were decidedly mainstream, so when The Sex Pistols became a media phenomenon in the UK, *Countdown*'s response was initially disparaging. I recall the show broadcasting a fleeting, but tantalizing clip of Johnny Rotten and his cohorts followed by a brief dismissal of the band's musical abilities. Like many other teenage viewers around Australia, I was immediately enthralled. I wanted to discover more about The Sex Pistols. My curiosity piqued; I wandered into 78 Records on Hay Street, at that time one of Perth's most important import record shops, and had a listen. I was hooked.

David McComb may or may not have had a similar response to the clip. What is not a matter of speculation is the fact that he became an early fan of Perth punk. He was particularly impressed by The Victims, a band fronted by Dave Faulkner who would later find pop success with The Hoodoo Gurus in the 1980s. A sixteen-year-old McComb wrote an effusively enthusiastic review of The Victims' last gig for *RAM* magazine in 1978 and penned the liner notes for The Victims' retrospective album in 1990:

> I saw the Victims play at salubrious Hernando's Hideaway in East Perth. They were inspirational in the simplest sense of the word. After that show I rushed home in

a state of adrenalin-fuelled adolescent ecstasy and breathlessly penned a piece of well-meaning drivel. It was printed in *RAM* magazine. I received a cheque for $23, and *RAM* told me 'we could use more of your stuff'. The only problem was, try as hard as I could, I found it impossible to write about music that didn't excite me – in the way the Victims did. Mediocrity provoked in me only a nauseous silence.

(cited in Walker, 1996, 48)

As Walker notes, McComb formed his own band instead of pursuing rock journalism. The Triffids soon became an integral part of Perth's punk scene, although the band embodied punk's DIY attitude more than its sonic characteristics.

The song 'Martyrs' appears on the band's first cassette. It's more Jonathan Richman than The Sex Pistols and its semi-ironic vitriol is directed towards Perth and its bland culture. It's an 'us and them' song that distinguishes discerning punks and Australia's 'moronic culture'. It's not hard to hear the influence of The Victims' 'Television Addict' in 'Martyrs' – both songs are up-tempo satires about popular culture; both alternate a sung/chanted chorus with semi-spoken verses more notable for their rhythmic delivery than their melodies.

Dave Faulkner recalls that Perth's punk scene, despite attracting modest media attention, was small:

Maybe 100 people? Maybe? It couldn't be much more than that. We were just trying to keep away the boredom and the feeling of being isolated and away from everything exciting in the world. Because all the music we loved was far away, it was never gonna come near us. We knew that much.

(quoted in Condon, 2020)

Commenting on the seminal Perth punk band, The Cheap Nasties, Douglas Galbraith argues that the band 'emerged from a virtual void of home-grown influence, succeeding in spite of the turgid local music scene and sparked by the sounds of overseas punk' (2019, 54).[1] Perhaps being part of a small subculture is a bit like being part of a persecuted religious sect, although I don't think anyone got killed for being a punk in Perth. The salient point here lies in the way Perth's punk scene inspired the young David McComb to take music seriously. Something exciting was happening in Perth, albeit on a small scale. The Triffids never embraced the shouty, overtly political tone of British punk music, but they absorbed its attitude towards mainstream culture and obviously embraced its DIY ethos.[2]

'Mark' (1978)

Before it was demolished to make way for the Forrest Chase complex in 1987, White Rider Records occupied Room 39 on the first floor of the Padbury Buildings in Perth's CBD. As I recall, the shop was shabby, but it specialized in import records from the UK and United States. I stumbled on White Rider while trying to track down albums by The Monkees in 1978 or 1979.

---

[1] Kim Salmon, the 'godfather of grunge', played in an early incarnation of this seminal Perth punk band.

[2] Perth punk often embraced a power pop sound. For example, see The Scientists' first self-titled album, the Manikins retrospective CD, and The Stems first album. In the mid- to late 1980s bands like The Quick and The Dead were more obviously related to early British punk and later incarnations of The Scientists along with Kim Salmon and The Surrealists developed a much harder sound.

At this time, the 'Prefab Four' were extremely popular thanks to reruns of their TV series, but it was impossible to get hold of the group's original albums (Arista released a greatest hits collection, but everything else was out of print). I discovered, to my delight, that the folks at White Rider would tape copies of unobtainable recordings, for a modest fee, if you supplied them with a few C90 cassette tapes.

The Triffids immortalized the proprietor of White Rider Records, Mark Edwards, on the band's first tape in 1978 (the band released six tapes between 1978 and 1981). The song begins with a simple guitar introduction, played by Phil Kakulas, and notable for its use of a wah-wah pedal (an effect that was, thankfully, not employed on any of the band's subsequent recordings). This is a piece of juvenile whimsy. McComb sketches a picture through a modest list of dubious biographical facts and personal observations. We learn Mark went to McComb's secondary school, Christ Church Grammar, that his shop is frequented by pretty girls and he, apparently, dislikes Florian Schneider, a member of the German band Kraftwerk.

McComb confesses he doesn't know much else about Mark but goes on to ad-lib a series of increasingly absurd observations about this mysterious figure. The song's significance for my purpose lies in its reference to one of the handful of import record shops in Perth in the late 1970s and 1980s, which also included 78 Records, DaDa Records, both located in the city and Mills Records in Fremantle. These stores played a key role in Perth's independent music scene and in the development of The Triffids. White Rider established its own record label and released singles by local bands, most notably The Scientists and The Rockets.

The Triffids sold their cassette albums through these independent record stores. That Perth could accommodate four or five import record shops during this era is significant as far as it shows that it was possible to hear what kinds of alternative sounds were being recorded and released 'over east' and in other parts of the world. In fact, these shops were an integral part of Perth's nascent punk/alternative eco-system which thrived between 1978 and 1987.

Today, Perth's CBD has very few heritage buildings. The city has a habit of demolishing its architectural heritage in the name of progress. The slightly seedy ambience of the Padbury buildings and edifices of a similar vintage have all but disappeared. While it would be absurd to claim that Perth's alternative scene was similar in scope and intensity to London's punk movement or the legendary 'downtown' assembly of artists in New York, it did provide basic infrastructure for those interested in leading a bohemian lifestyle. It was possible to rent cheap apartments, built in the 1920s, in and around the city. For example, Odd Fellows House and Plunkett House, both located on St George's Terrace and both victims of Perth's obsession with bland buildings made of steel and glass, attracted all manner of alternative types in the 1970s and 1980s, some of whom were artists, musicians and drug addicts.

'Nedlands by Night' (1979)

Well, will you see us walking around
Down to the river, down downtown
Late night delis, gardens, school bells
Yacht clubs, dances, shops, hotels

Andy Bennett claims that 'as a creative practice and as a form of consumption, music plays an important role in the narrativization of place, that is, in the way in which people define their relationship to local, everyday surroundings' (2005, 2). It is hardly surprising, then, that McComb wrote about his neighbourhood as an adolescent. He grew up in the salubrious suburb of Peppermint Grove, which is next to Nedlands, another affluent Perth suburb. 'Nedlands by Night' is not one of McComb's more memorable early compositions, but it highlights his teenage contempt for suburban complacency, a theme he intermittently explored throughout his career: 'Nedlands nights are safe and warm/Walking on the Nedlands lawn/No wildness to take your place/It's all too bad that you can't take space.'

Jon Stratton and Adam Trainer point out, 'every city has its myths' (2016), and one of Perth's biggest myths is that it's an extremely dull place, barely a metropolis. Consequently, the city supposedly lacked certain key prerequisites for the development of an alternative, independent music culture. Stratton remarks Perth lacked an inner-city area in the 1970s and 1980s (2005, 379). This observation is true in the sense that Perth had nothing akin to the downtown scene in lower Manhattan, or the bohemian inner-city suburbs of St Kilda, Fitzroy and Carlton in Melbourne, or Sydney's Newtown, Darlinghurst and Kings Cross districts – not that drug dealing, prostitution, cheap hotels, run-down apartments did not exist in areas like Northbridge, East Perth, North Perth and Highgate. Perth had its seedy side and, as I recall, it wasn't too hard to find its underbelly if you knew where to look.

Conceptually, the term 'inner city' was often synonymous with the word 'slum', although 'the distinction between city and suburb [in Australia] was never as definitive and inner-city areas were never the alien territory of American or British cities' (Howe, 1994, 142). In the 1980s, Perth possessed what urban policy researchers call a Night Time Economy (NTE). Alistair Sisson and Paul J. Maginn note that

> for much of its history it [Northbridge] was seen as being on the 'wrong side of the tracks'. In other words, Northbridge has long been a stigmatised place. The historical labelling and stigma levelled towards Northbridge is bound up in its social geography in that it has variously been a working-class neighbourhood, an enclave of Chinese, Jewish, Italian and Greek migrants, home to brothels, gambling dens and organised crime, and in more recent decades the nightlife epicentre of the city.
>
> (2018, 128)[3]

Perth, despite the relatively small size of its NTE spaces, possessed a vibrant alternative music scene, which spawned many of Australia's most critically acclaimed bands of the era, such as The Scientists and The Hoodoo Gurus, but how did this scene emerge? Was it just another form of teenage rebellion, a 1980s variant of earlier subversive Perth subcultures like the Bodgies and Widgies? (See Baker, 2018; Stratton, 1992 for more information about this group.)[4] Or was it a response to the conservative government of Sir Charles Court's triumphalist celebration of WA's 150th anniversary, as Julian G. Tompkin contends (2012)? Tompkin argues the West Australian punk scene railed against the state's prevailing obsession with football, farming, mining and bland entertainment, embodied in the now disgraced 'boy from Bassendean',

---

[3]   Northbridge became an official suburb, separate from Perth, in 1982.

[4]   The male members of this subculture were known as Bodgies and the females were called Widgies.

Rolf Harris who released his 'Back to WA' single on the eve of the Sesquicentenary Celebrations. Tompkin argues that punk's rejection of mainstream culture empowered the next generation of alternative musicians to do the same – with significant cultural ramifications for WA (2012). In a biographical sketch written for Mushroom Records around the time his solo album, *Love of Will,* was released, McComb characterized Perth as a cultural backwater:

> The Triffids were born to two teenagers in the Perth of the late '70s – a weird little historical and geographical interstice if ever there was one. This was the Perth of Norman Gunston, clear blue skies, watersports, all-night TV horrorthons, Hungry Jacks, the WAFL, the P76, the Noonkanbah episode, and more watersports. Politics was a distant rumble. There were slim pickings for precocious Stooges/Velvets/Eno fans. But anything was fair game to escape the heat and boredom of the world's most isolated capital city perched on a thin strip of arable coast between the desert and the Indian Ocean.
>
> (1994)

In this snapshot of his cultural context, McComb alludes to some of the more peculiar aspects of Australian culture, which require unpacking. Norman Gunston was the alter-ego of Australian comedian Gary MacDonald. His gormless Gunston persona was a nominal journalist who asked celebrities and public figures disarmingly naïve or absurdly invasive questions, often leaving them stunned, bemused or laughing nervously. His satire was often incisive and hilarious. In the late 1970s, one of the Perth TV stations used to run horror movies all night. These 'horrothons' showcased classic films from Universal Studios: *Dracula* (1931), *Frankenstein* (1931), *The Wolf Man* (1941) and so on. These films were supplemented with Hammer Horror films from the UK. As a migrant to Perth, I was astounded by all-night TV. In the 1970s and 1980s, UK TV stations went off the air at 10.30 pm! Hungry Jacks is the Australian franchise of Burger King, which was a novelty in Perth during the period McComb recalls in the quotation. The WAFL is an acronym for the West Australian Football League. The P76 was a grotesque, gas guzzling car made by Leyland Australia in the 1970s. It had a reputation for unreliability and spare parts were often hard to source. It stands as a symbol of hubris and excess. The 'Noonkanbah episode' was a 1979 dispute between the traditional indigenous owners of Noonkanbah Station, the Yungngora People and the WA government who wanted to mine the Nookanbah area for minerals (see Hawke and Gallagher, 1989).

The Perth scene may have been small, but it punched above its weight in terms of its contribution to the punk and post-punk scene in the late 1970s and 1980s. Rob Snarski, a member of Chad's Tree, one of Perth's most prominent alternative bands during this era, and later one of the co-founders of The Blackeyed Susans (with McComb and Phil Kakulas), describes his impression of Perth's 'inner-city' scene:

> The Shaftesbury was on the Northbridge side of Perth, over the Horseshoe Bridge, across from the offices of *The West Australian* newspaper. A couple of doors down was a blues bar called The Loaded Dog… and around the corner was a small hipster club called The Silver Slipper. Oddly, it didn't really feel like it was a happening strip; if anything it felt like a relatively dark and secluded, quiet part of town.
>
> (2017, 49)[5]

---

[5] The Horseshoe bridge is over the railway line, which divides the Perth CBD from the inner-city suburb of Northbridge.

While I share Snarski's memory of the scene, I don't think that inner-city music is exclusively created in geographical areas labelled as inner city. Alternative music isn't just about rundown buildings and sketchy places, but also about attitude and rebellion. It's got more to do with spirit than real estate. However, the difference between a supposedly conservative suburbia and a daring, radical inner city is significant in historical and critical studies of Australian popular music. To crudely summarize, Oz Rock, typified in the 1980s by mainstream bands like Cold Chisel, The Angels, Mondo Rock and Midnight Oil, thrived in suburban beer barns, whereas the alternative punk and post-punk bands were creatures of the inner city (Stratton, 2005; 2007; Turner, 1992; Walker, 1996). To invoke further stereotypes, Oz Rock fans were primarily so-called 'bogans' (Australian slang for uncouth, uneducated members of the working class). People who followed punk and post-punk bands such as The Triffids are perhaps best described, in the lexicon of urban theory, as 'cosmopolites' – 'students, artists, writers, musicians, and entertainers, as well as other intellectuals and professionals' (Gans, 1968, 66).[6] This binary division between the suburbs and inner city masks a more complex reality. Writing about the band, 'Dave Warner's from the Suburbs', Graeme Turner claimed that in Perth 'there is nothing but suburbs - no urban blight, no ghettos, no inner city bohemian areas' (1992, 23). As I recall suburbs like Midland, Morley, Maylands, Gosnells and Bassendean were gritty (there were no yacht clubs and all-night delis in these locations). Further, attending punk shows

---

6   The *OED* defines a cosmopolite as 'A "citizen of the world"; one who regards or treats the whole world as his or her country; one who has no national attachments or prejudices'. The word is often used as an antonym for patriot, so it carries a pejorative connotation in certain contexts.

in the late 1970s and early 1980s was not for the faint hearted given the large number of skinheads and neo-Nazis that were present at these gigs. It may not have protruded as far as some, but Perth's underbelly was real.

There are several quirky features about Perth's alternative music culture that are worth noting. First, a significant number of venues that supported Perth's alternative bands in the 1980s were located in the city's CBD and in adjacent areas like Northbridge, East Perth and Highgate. These venues included The East Perth Tavern, The Wizbar, The Shaftesbury Hotel, The Old Melbourne Hotel, The Red Parrott, The Northbridge Hotel, The Fitzgerald Hotel, Limbos Nightclub, The Equator, Rockwells, Hernando's Hideaway, Adrian's Nightclub and The Charles Hotel. That said, punters could also see alternative bands in smaller suburban venues like The Shenton Park Hotel, The Broadway Tavern and The Stoned Crow, where The Triffids began their career as a gigging band. Fremantle was another area that played host to bands that wrote and played their own songs. Some of these establishments, like The Shenton Park, one of the bastions of alternative music in Perth, also put on strip and lingerie shows, and bars like the Northbridge Hotel employed topless barmaids, too.

George Matzkov's book, *Way Out West: The West Australian Alternative Music Scene 1976–1989*, lists nearly 200 bands that played original music in Perth. Matzkov documents the variety of music produced by this scene on an accompanying CD. Many of these bands recorded and released their music on cassette and vinyl, some with the assistance of the local radio stations like 6UVS-FM and even the West Australian Government who ran a 'Demonstration Cassette Fund' between 1986 and 1987 (WA State Records Office: AU WA S29- cons3705 079).

While McComb lived in an affluent Perth suburb, his family made frequent trips to rural areas. McComb's brother John reminisced about these family outings in the slideshow presentation he made as part of The Triffids' Sydney Festival show in 2008 (*It's Raining Pleasure*, DVD, 2009). McComb's familiarity with the West Australian bush influenced his mature songs. His awareness of the contrast between the city and the country manifested in the next track in this location-inspired compilation of McComb songs.

'Farmers Never Visit Nightclubs' (1978, 1980)

Farmers nearly always have strong arms
They wake up early and drive around their farms
To see that their sheep have come to no harm
Farmers nearly always have strong arms, (strong arms)

Perth may have a reputation as a small, dull town, but it's a bona fide metropolis, an urban centre that offers many entertainment options to its inhabitants, including nightclubs. In the 1980s, none of the city's clubs possessed anything approaching the cultural cachet of a Studio 54 or a Mudd Club, but places like Gobbles, Beethoven's, Pinocchio's and Connections attracted a loyal clientele although most alternative types gave these 'daggy' establishments a wide berth.[7] McComb's satiric song declares emphatically that farmers never entered these establishments. Although comedic in tone, the song illuminates

---

[7]   On the Perth nightclub scene, see Panizza Allmark and Jon Stratton (2019, 714–23).

a significant divide in the culture of Western Australia (WA). WA covers a vast area of land, but most of the state's population live in the capital. The divide, though, between rural and urban folk continues to be stark and one of the most significant cultural and political fault lines in Australia.

McComb's family owned a farming property some 600 km south of Perth, so McComb was well placed to observe the differences between rural and urban people. It's a shame McComb isn't more specific about Perth's nightclubs. I'm not sure Perth punks visited nightclubs either, except for those venues that occasionally hosted live punk music (like Hernandos Hideaway and Adrian's, venues that loom large in the story of Perth punk). Nightclubs, certainly at the time McComb wrote the song, played dance music, predominantly disco, a genre not favoured by punks. Maybe farmers had more in common with punks than people seeking a hit of Saturday Night Fever.

The rural environment played a formative role in McComb's mature songwriting. Critics and commentators often remark on the 'light and space' in his music. McComb was conscious of this pastoral quality:

> Someone once told us that they never really understood us until they played one of our tapes in the country. Because I never thought of our music as being inner-city music at all, but we couldn't be dishonest and say we're really down-home either.
>
> (quoted in Walker, 2023, 162)

'Too Hot to Move' (1983, 1989)

Nothing prepared me for my first Perth summer. My family immigrated to one of the world's most isolated cities in August

1973. We arrived a few days shy of my eleventh birthday. While I was born in India, I'd spent most of my first decade living in Plaistow, East London, a dour working-class suburb near the West Ham United football ground. The sun shone down on Plaistow during summer, sometimes for as much as a week before the inevitable cloud-cover and drizzle would turn the sky to its natural setting: grey and overcast. I remember London winters more vividly. It snowed every year. The latter months of each year were bone-chillingly cold. It was always damp and icy, and night came early. Not that you could directly see it, but the sun set by 4.00 pm. East London was gloomy.

There is something otherworldly about the quality of light in Perth. For a recent arrival, it was as though the place was ensconced by a massively bright canopy of blue. David Whish-Wilson writes, 'Even in the unloveliest of suburbs, the sky arches from horizon to horizon, the sun passes unhurriedly across the usually blue sky, the stars and moon are clear at night' (2013, 22).

I remember my sense of wonder as I was driven from the Fremantle passenger terminal to Maylands via Stirling Highway, a road that hugs the Swan River as it winds towards the city, passing the sandstone University of Western Australia, and the old Swan Brewery among other notable landmarks. It was a cloudless spring day, warm, perhaps a little short of balmy.

I felt bewildered as I stepped into the weatherboard house rented by my mother's extended family for the first time. After London, Perth seemed unnervingly quiet. As the months rolled on, I noticed just how small the place was. Three-carriage suburban trains stopped at tiny one-platform stations. The streets of Maylands were almost empty. You could hear the squawks of birds over the sound of the sparse traffic and at night you could hear the high-pitched chirp of crickets compete with a chorus of croaks emitted by frogs.

Towards the end of October, the weather became hotter. By mid-November, the sun was intense. It generated a fierce, dry heat day-after-day. Concrete pavements and driveways absorbed the sun's scorching rays. It was impossible to walk comfortably on these surfaces without feeling as though the soles of your feet were on the point of burning. The temperature rarely dipped below 30 degrees, and it was not unusual to experience much hotter weather for longer stretches of time. Bore water drawn from under the land kept the lawns green in Maylands, mostly. You could always see patches of scorched grass. The subterranean source of irrigation also stained the concrete pathways an unsightly shit brown. How I hankered for snow that first summer. It felt impossible to do anything, which brings me to the song 'Too Hot to Think'.

As a Perth native, David McComb was all too familiar with the debilitating effects of Perth summers, which lead to a kind of existential despair, which Bleddyn Butcher describes as the city's ability to induce a torpor in its inhabitants (2011, 33). Obviously, people learn to cope with the relentless heat, but the song conveys something elemental about the struggle to keep one's sanity amid the West Australian capital's summer maelstrom. McComb wrote the song while he was still a teenager in the late 1970s, which adds to its poignant ability to convey the atmosphere of a world that no longer exists. Although McComb wrote the song in Sydney, it's a work that many Perth natives find compelling. Pat Monaghan, an early fan and supporter of the band, remarked:

> This guy's writing about where I live! He wasn't being funny or frivolous about it. He obviously felt uncomfortable about aspects of Perth but he also felt a deep affection … Or if he didn't like it, he appreciated the psychotic

nature of Perth, that beneath the façade of pastel there
was something darker, maybe.

(cited in Butcher, 2011, 131)[8]

The first scene of the song is set in a pub during a time when workers would consume as much alcohol as they could hold between the end of the working day, at 5.00 pm, and closing time at 6.00 pm. People colloquially referred to this period as the 5.00 o'clock swill. The song refers to a 'timer' ringing to signal closing time. And then there's the chorus:

> And from this window, I can see the street below
> I can hear the hit parade on the radio
> There're dirty dishes piling up in the sink
> But it's too hot to move, and it's too hot to think

Who listens to the hit parade on the radio these days? As the years go by, the song takes on an increasingly nostalgic tone. However, Perth summers are getting hotter and longer because of climate change, so the core of the tune's observations becomes even more pertinent to the experience of summer in McComb's hometown. You can probably still hear the lonesome bark of suburban hounds, and the despondent cries of mothers and their children bowed by the heat and haze. It's still too hot to move and too hot to think.

---

[8] Monaghan was a contributor to *Grok*, the West Australian Institute of Technology's student newspaper, which published some of the earliest writing about The Triffids. WAIT's 6NR radio station also played a significant role in the story of The Triffids, particularly through its influential program *Shake Some Action*. In 1980, the show held a songwriting competition, which The Triffids won, earning studio time and the pressing of a 45rpm single. This victory led to the release of 'Stand Up' b/w 'Farmers Never Visit Nightclubs'.

Musically, this song is indestructible. It works in its original low-fi form and takes on a grandeur on the version that appears on *The Black Swan*. My favourite version is harder to track down. David and Graham Lee performed an acoustic rendition of the song for Swedish radio in the 1990s, which is sublime. Except for subtle reverb, David's voice is unadorned; Graham's pitch-perfect harmony enhances the song's country flavour. The performance is intimate. I can only speculate what the band's Nordic fans made of this slice of West Australian life.

'Hometown Farewell Kiss' (1987)

A certain ambivalence marks the songs McComb wrote about Perth. 'Hometown Farewell Kiss', another key song on *Calenture*, sees its narrator hovering above his hometown as it burns. Is he dreaming? Is he a ghost? Either way, he's kept a cognitive map of the city in his head as he roams around – he knows this town; he knows how its complacent suburbs can stifle ambition. Saying goodbye, he returns to kiss the place:

> Higher, let the flames grow higher
> Erase my name from your lips as we kiss
> Higher, let the flames grow higher
> Now there's one soul less on your fiery lips

This delirious vision of Perth burning down certainly fits with the theme of *Calenture*, but it repeats the ambivalence McComb expresses about his hometown in earlier songs like 'Nervous Side of Town' (which appears on 'tape 5' in 1980) and the better-known 'Spanish Blue' – a song composed in Papua New Guinea, but which resonates with Perth's reputation as a complacent city (Stratton, 2009).

Nothing happens here, nothing gets done
But you get to like it
You get to like the beating of the sun
The washing of the sun in Spanish Blue

Stratton interprets 'Spanish Blue' as a song that depicts the 'easygoing hedonism of suburban, utopian, idyllic Perth' (2009, 37). In contrast, he notes,

> 'Nervous Side of Town' couples an almost jaunty, sing-along tune with lyrics suggestive of a darker, more problematic aspect of cultural life. The lyrics themselves, especially in the second verse, suggest the suburban neurosis that Jonathan Richman mined in his first album, *The Modern Lovers* (1976).
>
> (2009, 41)

The narrator of 'Hometown Farewell Kiss' is not so much nervous as contemptuous and perhaps unwilling to pay the price of living in an idyllic paradise (if Perth is such a place): 'Now it blazes for me house by house/And my legs they buckle under me/But I don't mind, I sing the old song of joy/For I know why and why it had to be.' McComb's vocation is not compatible with suburbia. Nothing gets done if you are seduced by the sun, sand and surf. Better to burn the whole place down lest you get sucked into the trap of contentment.

Unfortunately, McComb's calling turned him into a vagabond, a rootless wanderer who, in the song 'Vagabond Holes', issues a desperate plea to find something to fill the empty spaces carved out by his itinerant lifestyle. Once again, the song deals with love lost because of wanderlust. As harrowing as the lyrics are, speaking as they do about addiction, poverty, age and catatonic depression, it's the chilling scream that ends the song that best conveys McComb's increasingly precarious state of being, which makes suburban self-satisfaction look like a viable lifestyle choice.

'American Sailors' (1989)

This unusually short song, which is paired with 'Too Hot to Move' on *The Black Swan*, evokes a period in the 1980s when the American Navy regularly docked in the port city of Fremantle, so its sailors could get some rest and recreation. The weary mariners would hit the pubs, clubs and brothels with gusto. Hotels would routinely welcome these visitors with signs advertising topless barmaids and cheap alcohol. What could go wrong?

'American Sailors' is a bit like an imagist poem, or perhaps a haiku. Imagism, according to M. H. Abrams, 'was a poetic movement that flourished in England, and even more vigorously in America, between the years 1912 and 1917' (1971, 77). 'The Red Wheelbarrow' by William Carlos Williams is perhaps the best-known example of this genre. Typically, these poems present 'the writer's response to a visual object or scene' and are marked by an economy of language (1971, 78). McComb's song is only five lines long, but its image of the narrator's sisters 'bathing their shoulders in the night air' conveys the sexual *frisson* that permeated those summer encounters between the visiting sailors and the young women of Perth. Although it is impossible to determine the conscious influence of these poetic forms on him, McComb was certainly familiar with them as a creative writing student at WAIT. Abrams' book, incidentally, was required reading for all students enrolled in the first year of the BA [English] degree at WAIT. The song evokes another slice of Perth life from a bygone era while signalling McComb's explicitly literary sensibility.

'OBH' (posthumously published poem, 2009)

While the farmers of Western Australia may not have patronized Perth's nightclubs in the 1980s, they regularly lodged at the Ocean Beach Hotel (OBH) in the early decades of the twentieth century. American sailors also took refuge at the OBH during the Second World War courtesy of the US Navy, which leased the building temporarily.

Located on the corner of Eric Street and Marine Parade in Cottesloe, the OBH was built in 1907 and opened the following year. This iconic building loomed large in the culture of Perth during the 1980s. David McComb's poem 'OBH' captures its once-seedy atmosphere:

> Lead-enriched exhaust fumes,
> pizza belch and spittle resin do battle
> with stiff sea breeze and sand
> particles whipped into flight

The McComb family home was within walking distance from Cottesloe Beach and the OBH, so while David may not have been a regular patron of the establishment, he knew it well enough to comment on its place within Perth's cultural scene. For McComb, the OBH is a masculine space ('singlets twang with the sweaty discharge of male toil'). This assessment tallies with my memory of the pub, but only up to a point, since my visits were fleeting and restricted to the section of the hotel that overlooked the beach. Certainly, the OBH was as rough as the sea that's visible from its front bar, but it functioned as a meeting place for a range of subcultures: on any summer's evening, as the sun dipped below the horizon, you could find surfies, bikies and even alternative types, drinking, smoking, chatting and scoring drugs.

3   The making of *Truckload of Sky: The Lost Songs of David McComb, Volume 1*

Derrida once remarked that friendship begins with the possibility of survival, since one friend must, almost inevitably, outlive the other (Derrida, 1997, 14). In their editor's introduction to Derrida's posthumous collection of eulogies for his deceased friends, *The Work of Mourning* (2001), Pascale-Anne Brault and Michael Naas point out that 'even when friends die together, or rather, at the same time, their friendship will have been structured from the very beginning by the possibility that one of the two would see the other die, and so, surviving, would be left to bury, to commemorate, and to mourn' (2001, vii). This structural law of friendship, while ensuring that questions of remembrance and mourning are always an integral part of friendship, also raises several practical and ethical problems, which Derrida identifies in his eulogies. For example, he notes the paradox of mourning: 'To speak of the dead is to expose oneself to their absence, to the irreplaceable singularity of the one who is no more' (Derrida, 2001, 107).

This paradox will be familiar to most people who have written a eulogy. Derrida also asks whether it's possible to represent the dead properly through words. In commemorating someone, we invoke their memory, yet simultaneously reduce their singularity to something that we can speak or write about: 'How can we do justice to the other, to the one who is gone, through the words we choose to remember them by?' (Derrida, 2001 119). He also points out that to 'mourn is to engage with the other without assimilating them entirely, without making them an image of our own' (Derrida, 2001, 124). In other words, how do we preserve their singularity without imposing our own frameworks of understanding on their life? Mourning for a friend, Derrida suggests, involves confronting our own mortality since 'in the death of the other, we also encounter the horizon of our own finitude' (Derrida, 2001, 152).

There is a connection between hauntology and mourning because the departed other never fully disappears. They persist as a spectre, shaping the mourner's life through memories, dreams and the unfinished dialogue between them. Hauntology also redefines friendship by emphasizing the trace and the impossibility of closure. The spectral friend – whether alive or dead – remains an ungraspable other, constantly shaping the present through their absence. While David McComb was undoubtedly unlucky in love, he gathered a loyal group of friends, family and fans who care for his legacy. These ethical and philosophical considerations will provide the implicit theoretical frame for the following account of the making of *Truckload of Sky*.

In 1985, as most fans of The Triffids know, the band appeared on the front cover of the *New Musical Express* with the headline: '1985: the year of The Triffids?' That tentative prophecy never came to pass, and while McComb has undoubtedly achieved a degree of posthumous success, his friends and fans continue to lament the fact that his work is not better known. They have also, over the last few decades, remembered him through staging concerts, exhibitions and, more recently, by recording some of his lost songs. The following account of the making of *Truckload of Sky* engages, sometimes directly and at other times implicitly, with Derrida's remarks on the ethics of friendship and mourning that frame this chapter.

The Triffids reissued and remastered their back catalogue in the first decade of the twenty-first century. And as we have seen, friends of McComb, such as Niall Lucy and Bleddyn Butcher, have either written or edited books about his life and career. The surviving members of The Triffids have staged concerts in Australia and Europe, featuring guest vocalists and instrumentalists. Robert McComb told me that nobody in the band felt like playing David's music in the immediate aftermath of his death:

> But when the opportunity came to give it a try, it changed our perspective. We realised that playing these songs was a way to keep Dave's art alive and it was also something we enjoyed doing together. It became a meaningful and enjoyable way to honour his legacy.
>
> (Personal Interview, 2024)

In 2006, two passionate Belgian fans of the band, Jo Lijnen and Liesbeth Janssens, organized an exhibition of Triffids memorabilia at *Kunstencentrum Belgie* in Hasselt. They invited the band to attend. Graham Lee recalls:

> When we first started playing the songs in Belgium, we were a bit hesitant. An art exhibition, featuring posters and memorabilia, was set up by some old fans at their art centre in Hasselt, and they invited us over. They even covered the costs for us and our families, and we stayed in a beautiful Art Deco mansion in the centre of town. We had the chance to rehearse on the stage where we

would later perform. They suggested that we might want to play some of Dave's songs, and it felt almost disrespectful not to, so we decided to go ahead. As soon as we began playing, it became clear that this was how we can best remember Dave – through the music he left us. It all made sense, even though we might have been a bit rough around the edges. There was an incredible spirit in the room, and it felt surreal to be rehearsing while the art gallery was being set up around us.

(Personal Interview, 2024)

Truckload of Sky is part of this broader and monumental effort to solidify McComb's legacy as an important Australian artist. The care and attention to detail that went into the production of the album is a testament to the respect McComb's friends and collaborators feel for him.

Graham Lee and Robert McComb told me they were both in possession of some of David's belongings (journals, essays, demo cassettes and so on) but the impetus for the *Truckload of Sky* album came from the reissue of the band's back-catalogue by Domino Records. John Dyer, who runs the label, helped to ensure the creative vision for the reissue was upheld, even allowing the use of a silver cover that significantly increased production costs for the vinyl re-releases of The Triffids' singles. As Graham Lee recalls, 'John Dyer emailed me to discuss his position and asked if we could proceed without the silver cover. I replied that it wouldn't really make sense to do that' (Personal Interview, 2024). Despite initial hesitations, Dyer managed to secure the resources, surprising everyone by announcing, 'We have silver' (Lee 2024). His help extended beyond this, facilitating the release of a box set of rarities, which required revisiting the band's archive. Lee recalled he discovered tracks he hadn't heard before while compiling the set.

While researching for a now hideously rare and overpriced 10 CD box of rarities in the first decade of this century, I would stumble across full blown masterpieces I'd never heard, recorded on a cassette with an unplugged electric guitar while others slept, perhaps with his dogs for company, or Bryant Gumble and Katie Couric [Hosts of the American 'Today' show in the 1990s] faintly droning on low volume in the background. He'd sketch instructions–'alternative bass line for … string section for … new middle 8 for …' I didn't put any of these treasures on the box set because I thought one day something might happen.

(24 July 2023, FB Post)

In 2018, Graham and Robert assembled a group of musicians to record some of these 'lost songs' which came from three sources: David McComb's cassette recordings, demos and live recordings he made with his last band, costar and a session recorded on a four-track reel-to-reel machine at Lee's home in the late 1990s. McComb did not live long enough to record these songs professionally. Robert McComb recalled he possessed

a couple of cassettes with songs like 'It's Good to Be Home', which was a demo Dave had recorded. There were a few other scraps we haven't yet put together, but the ones that ended up on the record were relatively easy to work with since they were complete and required minimal additional effort. Arranging the songs was great fun. For example, we had a live recording of 'Kiss Him (He's History)' which we knew could be used as-is. For most of the other tracks, we had to figure out the instrumentation.

(Personal Interview, 2024)

He also pointed out that 'most of the recordings on *Truckload of Sky* were structurally sound and fairly complete' (2024). Graham adds that 'we could hear what he was trying to do. He had arrangements, but sometimes it was hard to figure out the words' (2024). McComb prepared meticulous notes for most of his recordings, but Lee recalled he did not leave behind detailed instructions for how he envisioned the songs that appear on *Truckload of Sky*: 'Our familiarity with his style and preferences helped us navigate the process. We were just trying to play them in a way that Dave wasn't tempted to strike us with a thunderbolt from above' (2024). Robert recalled:

> With Dave, there was a clear contrast between his approach to songs like 'Red Pony' [the first track on the *Treeless Plain* album] and our process. For 'Red Pony', Dave would come in with a definitive vision – like specifying that the song would have strings and a particular arrangement. He was adventurous, but always had a clear direction. On the other hand, without Dave around, we were more cautious. We aimed to respect the essence of the song and not overshadow it. We didn't want the music to be too distracting or detract from the core of Dave's songs. It's a cliché, but we're serving the song and doing our best to make sure the lyrics get across, which is the main thing with Dave's songs. We didn't want to be too distracting with the music.
>
> (Personal Interview, 2024)

Phil Kakulas, who co-produced the album with Graham Lee, also wrestled with recording McComb's songs in his absence:

> I did feel pressure and responsibility to not fuck the songs up. I know there were occasions when people would say, 'What would Dave do?' and I always appreciated that, but

we had to adhere to Dave's own rule that the song always
comes first. I'd like to think if we did that, it would have
made Dave happy.

(2020)

Some tracks required more experimentation than others. In its
original demo form, 'Make Believe We're Not in Hell' sounded,
to Graham's ears, a bit like a prog-rock song, 'it was jerky, a bit
like XTC' (Lee 2024). Robert recalled that

> we played in various ways – slowed down, sped up, and
> so on. It wasn't until we were actually recording it that
> Graham suggested we strip it back to just piano and
> vocals. Of course, a bit of guitar found its way in, but the
> idea of approaching it from this completely different
> angle was revealing. From the first lines, it was clear that
> this was the right approach.

(McComb, 2024)

Rehearsing together felt natural for the band members, who
had known each other's playing styles for years. 'We realised
that first afternoon of rehearsal that the chemistry was right',
says Lee. 'It was smooth sailing from the start.' The relaxed
atmosphere of the sessions enabled the players and vocalists
to enjoy their time in the studio with no real expectations
beyond making good recordings.

The vocalists included established artists like Rob Snarski,
a close friend and a key collaborator in The Black Eyed Susans,
and people like J. P. Shilo and Simon Breed who had sung with
the surviving members of The Triffids in the past. Lee explained
how Alex Gow, who was more connected with the local scene,
introduced Romy Vager, who hadn't previously been part of
The Triffids' world. They also brought in Angie Hart. Robert
noted that 'we were aiming for more female representation

in the line-up, rather than just a group of old white guys'
(McComb 2024).

The collaborative spirit and ease of the process showed
how much love and care went into crafting *Truckload of Sky*,
a heartfelt tribute to Dave McComb's legacy. McComb once
remarked that 'writing a song's really easy, arranging it is what
makes it special' (quoted in Walker, 2023, 162). As we shall see
in the next chapter, the songs on the album, while reprising
many aspects of McComb's artistry, are darker than his work
with The Triffids. Phil Kakulas comments that 'the stuff from the
90s is a lifetime away from that early stuff. His turn of phrase;
there's a particular sensibility that is quite unique. But there's
a whole lot of water under the bridge. There's a definitely a
bitterness there' (quoted in Dwyer, 2020).

McComb often drew on his personal life in his songwriting.
He made no secret of this practice, so it is tempting to read
his work autobiographically. Regarding the songs he wrote
for *Born Sandy Devotional*, he admitted, in a personal letter
to a friend, that 'I'm starting to view a lot of my work as
autobiographical, especially the new stuff. I can't pretend
otherwise, the songs on the new album are as honest as I can
get, while still having a narrative or cinematic feel' (Quoted in
Butcher, 2011, 250). But songs have other dimensions that we
cannot reduce to autobiography, regardless of their origins
in personal experience. A song, once released, becomes an
autonomous entity – a work of art that will attract a variety of
readings and interpretations.

While it would be churlish to dismiss McComb's comments
about the autobiographical dimension of his songs, it's
important to remember that he often wrote in character:
the suicide in 'Tarrilup Bridge,' the broken-hearted farmer in
'New Year's Greetings,' the frozen fossil in 'Jerdacuttup Man,'

to cite some of the most obvious examples of this aspect of McComb's songwriting. He also embraced the dramatic monologue structure in songs like 'Stolen Property' and 'Field of Glass'. Having a range of singers voice McComb's 'lost songs' heightens their dramatic, character-driven qualities. He obviously recognized the theatricality of his work since Jill Birt sang some of McComb's best character-driven songs.

The singers on *Truckload of Sky* are all accomplished songwriters, but they showcase their interpretative talents on McComb's 'lost' songs, which are dark, sometimes harrowing, and on par with his previous work. For me, one of the greatest strengths of *Truckload of Sky* lies in its presentation of McComb's songs as mini-plays, vignettes about existential despair, mortality, treachery and revenge. It's as though a diverse bunch of characters, from different walks of life, are marooned in a lonely place, all attuned to the same mood, which they grapple with in different emotional registers, vocal timbres and tones. This makes *Truckload of Sky* much more than a mere tribute record. It deals with weighty themes: despair, regret and impending death, topics that become increasingly poignant for McComb's original fans who are now amid their own third act dramas.

On a more celebratory note, the album gives artists like London singer-songwriter, Simon Breed, and Alex Gow of the ARIA award-winning band, Oh Mercy, the opportunity to share their enthusiasm of McComb's music. They both cite him as inspiring their own careers. Gow's favourite album is *Born Sandy Devotional*, which he describes as 'mysterious, romantic, menacing, evocative and smart' (2016). McComb's part of the tradition I described earlier in this book, and artists like Gow and Breed, among others, are still conversing with his ghost.

4 Reading David McComb's lost songs

Truckload of Sky: The Lost Songs of David McComb is, for me, an astonishing album. It shows that David McComb's songwriting prowess remained undiminished, even in the face of ill health. The album features some of his most complex and nuanced lyrics, showcasing a depth and complexity that stands out in his body of work. As I will illustrate, the songs on this album, unsurprisingly, echo various aspects of McComb's earlier work, creating another portal into the past. However, the self-referential nature of these songs is less striking than the way McComb, in his maturity, revisits his favourite themes. The love songs, for instance, are steeped in bitterness and cynicism, grappling with toxic relationships, overwhelming emotions of hatred, and a thirst for revenge. The songs that confront his health struggles and the looming shadow of death are harrowing. There's also something profoundly moving about hearing his older writing voice emerge through new material, as though he's speaking to us from beyond the grave, addressing a now older fanbase, many confronting their own mortality.

Truckload of Sky is serious in its thematic content, yet it surprises and uplifts in unexpected ways. For fans, it is heartening to see that McComb's friends and musical comrades invested time and effort to polish a collection of songs that were never fully realized in the studio. These songs, drawn from rough cassette demos, live recordings and various drafts of lyrics, have been lovingly brought to life. In a sense, *Truckload of Sky* serves as McComb's second solo album, despite his voice being absent from the recordings. It is also fascinating to hear other artists interpret McComb's 'lost' songs; as a songwriter, he would undoubtedly appreciate hearing his music filtered through the artistry of such a diverse group of performers, some of whom had never met him. Robert McComb recalled that 'Dave often introduced songs with a tongue-in-cheek comment, like saying he wrote a song for Willie Nelson, which showed he thought his songs could be sung by other artists' (Personal Interview, 2024). And Graham Lee remembers a time when he received a visit from Dave and Will Akers carrying

> bags and bags of cassettes and reams of paper. They poured this all on my floor, and Dave said, I want other people to sing my songs. We've been going through them, and these are the ones that we think can be done by other people. And it was all sorts of things. Dave did want his songs to be done by other people.
>
> (Personal Interview, 2024)

Of course, many artists have recorded McComb's songs throughout the years.[1] However, *Truckload of Sky* takes a

---

[1] Unsurprisingly, several artists have recorded McComb's most celebrated song, 'Wide Open Road'. Apart from 1980s bands like The Church and Weddings, Parties, Anything, The Panics and Missy Higgins have all attempted to put their own stamp on this iconic composition. Other notable covers of McComb songs include 'Bury Me Deep in Love' by Jimmy Little and Kylie Minogue and 'Raining Pleasure' by Texas Tea. The problem with most of these recordings is that they compare unfavourably to the original versions.

unique approach by giving voice to his 'lost' songs in a manner that is truly compelling. In the analysis that follows, I will delve into each song, paying particular attention to how they resonate with the themes and motifs that I have identified as distinctive features of McComb's writing: his obsession with toxic love, the use of religious language and symbolism, his ambivalent relationship with home and his deep love of the pop music tradition, which his collaborators evoke in several tracks. The album is bittersweet and unsettling, reminding us that while McComb is no longer with us, his spirit haunts the album. *Truckload of Sky* is not merely an act of remembrance; it represents the fulfilment of a promise made by his friends and colleagues to keep his spirit alive.

The album begins with a trilogy of bitter songs about friendship, intimacy and betrayal. To call these tracks love songs, though, betrays their complexity.

'Kneel So Low'

'Perception', writes Oliver Sacks, 'is never purely in the present' (2008, 156). We recall memories of previous experiences with each new perception. Certainly, my experience of listening to *Truckload of Sky* was shaped by my memories of listening to The Triffids over a long period of time. I can't help hearing the traces of McComb's previous work in his 'lost' songs (recurrent images, song structures, musical motifs and so on). This is especially the case with the album's first track, 'Kneel So Low', which is sung by Romy Vager.

Written in the 1990s, possibly as a contender for McComb's solo album, *Love of Will* (1994), 'Kneel So Low' reminds me of 'The Seabirds', the opening track on *Born Sandy Devotional,* which I explicated in some detail in Chapter 1. Both songs use nautical imagery and share a 'cold opening' in the sense that the lyrics and music come in at the same time. They also feature insistent, melodic guitar motifs, but they offer two very different experiences of the eerie in Fisher's sense of the term.

The eerie, you will recall, is defined by an absence where presence is expected, or a presence where absence is expected. It is tied to questions of agency – who or what is behind this? – and a deep, unsettling feeling of the unknown. Ruins, landscapes, oceans can be eerie when we detect some unseen entity that generates unsettling affects. McComb's music, I have argued, often uses this hauntological trope. Put another way, the eerie generates an unsettling atmosphere, attunes us to a disturbing mood.

The ocean, in both sets of lyrics, conjures an existential abyss. The ocean becomes increasingly dangerous the further one ventures into it. The vastness of the ocean subsumes the individual. Whereas the ocean in 'The Seabirds' is both a literal and symbolic image, 'Kneel So Low' uses the ocean as a metaphor for the narrator's inner world, which is as hazardous as any material space.

Romy Vager, of RGV, sings 'Kneel So Low' in a restrained voice, which heightens the song's scornful tone. The character Vager embodies exhorts a former lover (or intimate friend) to 'take a leap out on *my* ocean', suggesting perhaps that this erstwhile paramour dive into the singer's revengeful state of mind. She asks her lover/friend to swim into a dangerous space where 'one's feet no longer touch the sand' where she then imagines them drowning while thinking of her. The song explores how relationships can mutate over time ('friendship becomes disease') and resonates with Derrida's observation that every friendship 'slips into enmity, every declaration of fraternity contains the seed of discord' (Derrida, 1997, 231).

The tension between what remains unforgettable and what has become unlovable creates an eerie paradox, where memory and loss coexist in a way that disturbs the natural order of relationships. The image of someone 'crawling out of the sea' to 'beg scraps of love' suggests a return from the depths, almost like a revenant coming back from the dead. This is a powerful evocation of the eerie – something that should remain gone or forgotten instead returns in a degraded, pitiful form. This return is not a redemption but a desperate, haunting presence that insists on acknowledgement, much like the eerie presence of ghosts or unresolved traumas.

The last lines of the song introduce the idea of a 'blade' buried in the singer – a symbol of betrayal and deep-seated hurt. This grudge, which the speaker cannot let go, keeps the past alive in a way that is eerie. The unresolved nature of this betrayal lingers like a ghost, haunting the present and preventing closure. This haunting tract sets the tone for the rest of the album, which wades into increasingly treacherous waters.

'Kiss Him (He's History)'

You can hear McComb's love of 1960s girl group songs in this track (and traces of the first version of 'Not the Marrying Kind' I discussed in Chapter 1). The exquisite harmonies and the call and response backing vocals are a male version of the sounds made by groups like The Shirelles and The Ronettes, but this is not a teenage love song. Bleddyn Butcher claims McComb loved 'the torrid intensity of those songs, their breathless all-or-nothing extremity' (2011, 31). McComb himself spoke authoritatively about the genre in an interview he recorded for Swedish radio (1991), indicating that he feels some people dismiss the genre as kitsch or camp because they can't cope with the emotional intensity of girl group songs: 'It's not a game. I hear some real emotion in that music' (1991). Apparently, McComb never lost his love for girl groups. On this track he puts his own spin on the form by eschewing emotional intensity for low-key calculation. While McComb is attuned to the conventions and nuances of various musical traditions, he rarely writes generic songs. Rather, he introduces an element of surprise that makes the listener sit up and take notice.

Rob Snarski's smooth croon amplifies the song's cold, manipulative sentiment. His vocals convey the song's extremity through an almost matter-of-fact delivery. In today's parlance, we might say 'Kiss Him' is a song about 'love bombing' – that is, a form of psychological abuse that uses attention and flattery as a weapon. After a period of overwhelming praise, the love bomber will typically discard their plaything and as McComb sang on The Triffids' first album, the only good plaything is 'a dead ringer for the real thing' – this reference reminds us that McComb's love songs frequently express a suspicion of insincerity in matters of the heart. In 'Place in the Sun' he sings 'Let's not talk about love/that's just something you feel for a dog or a cat'. 'Kiss Him' and 'Spanish Blue' are songs that express irony through marrying dark lyrics with music that communicates a contrary emotion. In 1985, McComb remarked that he'd become wary of this songwriting strategy:

> We used to have songs that I thought were the most depressing songs ever. Like 'Close to the Sun', which was

a really in-the-pits song, and people used to say, What a great surf song![2] That reminds me of the beach! And I thought, 'God, we've really failed there', because I was trying for an irony.

(McComb quoted in Walker, 2023, 163)

The lyrics of 'Kiss Him' describe a manipulative and emotionally detached approach to relationships. The singer advises someone on how to play with a lover's emotions: don't do things by half measures, the cynical mentor croons. If you are going to kiss your victim, make sure it feels like the real thing: 'keep them gasping for air'. And if you're going to drive them, well, 'drive him *all* the way home'. When you leave them heartbroken and alone, the pain will be intensified by the illusion of love. The overall tone of the lyrics is cynical, implying that love and relationships are more about manipulation and less about true emotional intimacy. The repetition of the refrain, 'Kiss him, he's history', strengthens the idea that it's possible to use love as a weapon to allure and later heartlessly dispose of one's lover. Rob Snarski's phrasing gives the song a seductive, romantic air, and it is the clash between his vocal presentation and the cynicism of the lyrics that gives this song its power. Ultimately, the lyrics convey a cold and calculated approach to romance, where the aim is not love or connection, but power and emotional control.

The song changes its tone during the long fade-out from the 3.51-minute mark. The distorted guitar chords convey the narrator's contemptuous attitude towards love, thereby closing the gap between the cynical sentiment of the lyrics and the romantic musical backing.

---

[2]   I suspect McComb is referring to 'Place in the Sun'. 'Close to the Sun' is probably a printing error in Walker's text.

'Second Nature'

You can hear a female voice duetting with McComb on the original demo of this song (which is a very basic guitar and vocal cassette recording). So, it's fitting that Angie Hart's distinctive Australian accent lends a conversational tone to the lyrics. Her phrasing creates the impression of eavesdropping on an intimate conversation. Put more formally, the lyrics follow a free verse style, with loose, colloquial rhythms. The irregular metre creates a feeling of natural speech, which builds an emotional and reflective tone. Some stanzas have more structured rhyme and rhythm, but overall, the lyrics seem to prioritize meaning and mood over strict metrical form. For example, the first verse ('Did you dream of this loneliness/Or is this what we've travelled so far for') sounds like a question lingering in the air.

The song revisits some of McComb's favourite themes: fidelity, or the impossibility of fidelity, and the promise of salvation through love. The narrator questions whether her experience of love may have always been illusion: 'Is the way things are the way things always were?' Perhaps the couple were just kidding themselves all along. McComb uses Christian imagery to further explore the theme of disappointment and disillusion in human relationships. The line 'Oh Jesus made a promise/He did his best to keep it' references the promise of salvation, but also suggests that Jesus broke his divine promise. If this is so, what hope for mere mortals? Indeed, the phrase 'we did not burn out the way the good lord thought we would' implies a disconnect between divine expectations and human reality.

The refrain 'it's second nature to hurt someone' reinforces this proposition, suggesting that humans are inherently flawed, and the impulse to hurt is an integral part of our psychology. And if this instinctual compulsion constrains us, it becomes impossible to believe in moral purity. By describing the act of holding the rosary tightly while acknowledging the difficulty of being 'a good woman', the lyrics address the emotional toll of trying to live up to unrealistic moral standards, reflecting the struggle between the desire for goodness and the pressures or realities that make it challenging to achieve. The song reminds me of Joy Division's 'Love Will Tear Us Apart' in how routine and everyday stress erode romantic love. McComb's composition highlights the tension between spiritual ideals and human reality, questioning why inherently flawed people make sacred promises.

Graham Lee proffers a more prosaic reading of the song's lyrics. Noting that it was written in the early 1990s when McComb was trying to secure a recording contract in the UK, he thinks the song is 'about him locking horns with the music establishment and not getting anywhere, and them treating him like an old scummy rag. It's quite vicious and mean' (quoted in Dwyer, 2020).

'Lucky for Some'

This is a harrowing composition, inspired, no doubt, by McComb's ill-health towards the end of his life; he had a heart transplant in May 1996. The song's narrator is staring up at a ceiling fan from his hospital bed while ruminating on how fickle life can be. Some get lucky and avoid the worst pitfalls of existence, while others, randomly, suffer. The song resonates with Hamlet's most famous line about suffering the 'slings and arrows of outrageous fortune'. Life is essentially a crapshoot, and the wheel of fortune turns unpredictably.

The song also captures a fragile and fearful psychological state. The narrator is lonely, marooned in hospital. He hears the voice and footsteps of his lover and while the thought of her embrace gives him momentary solace, he cannot be sure whether she is there. This suggests he is in a dream-like state, making it difficult to apprehend reality. He inhabits a restless, liminal state between sleep and wakefulness, and the morning light brings no respite from the ghostly forces that haunt him during the night. The images and sounds (the bed, the fan, the tiles, the shadows, the morning light) take on an ominous quality, which J. P. Shilo intensifies with his deeply unsettling performance, which, for me, channels the spirit of David McComb.

If anyone can channel McComb, it's J. P. Shilo – his vocal tone, timbre and phrasing make him sound uncannily like the author of 'Lucky for Some'. This is not to diminish Shilo's talent. He possesses a sense of drama that he conveys through a nuanced performance, building tension and unease. Shilo breaks into a blood-curdling howl towards the end of the song and his repetition of the phrase, 'lucky for some', emphasizes the cyclical nature of fate and the inevitable encounter with mortality. This song sent chills and shivers up my spine. For me, this is the standout track on the album, testifying to the power of music in generating unsettling, spectral effects. The almost palpable sense of McComb's pain, as channelled by Shilo, is deeply and mysteriously powerful. Indeed, witnessing Shilo's performance at the Perth International Festival in 2016 inspired me to investigate the relationship between hauntology and music. His deeply affecting execution of McComb's music evoked an unsettling sense of making the absent artist present. It was as though he was functioning as a medium.

Shilo told me he naturally faces both technical and ethical considerations when performing songs by deceased artists.

Shilo, while an impressive artist in his own right, often pays tribute to his former colleague and band-mate Rowland S. Howard, as a part of 'Pop Crimes: The Songs of Rowland S. Howard' a tribute to the guitarist of The Birthday Party – by inhabiting Rowland's iconic shrieking guitar lines that underpin the shows, along with distinctive vocal contributions. He's also recorded numerous songs written by Jeffrey Lee Pierce across three volumes of 'The Jeffrey Lee Pierce Sessions Project' in tribute of the late The Gun Club maestro.

'When I perform Dave's Songs', Shilo tells me, 'I try to imagine how he might have done them if he was still in his prime. That's my motivation. I want to respect the Artist and honour their Vision especially when I'm working from their rough demos or sketches that hadn't fully had the chance to come to life yet' (Personal Interview, 2024). This desire to respect the Artist involves paying specific attention to the many idiosyncratic nuances of their vocal stylings, both in tone and execution:

> When I listen to the way Dave sings, I noticed he often attacks the first syllable of the line in this well-rounded, almost bell-like tone, and lets the rest of the line trail off like smoke. My main motto is 'Serve the Song'. It's about getting out of the way. Let the spirit of the music carry me – through me. I don't want to impose myself on the song – just be fully immersed in it.
>
> (Personal Interview, 2024)

Shilo's performative approach to 'Lucky for Some' shows his deep commitment to becoming a vessel for the music rather than a dominant performer. By submerging himself so deeply in the material, Shilo aims to let the music speak through him without interference, creating an uncanny affect, which resonates with an almost literal form of hauntological performance.

'So Good to Be Home'

'Rob Snarski sings a song that is, at least on the surface, as happy and uncomplicated as Dave's songs get'. This description of 'So Good to Be Home' (published on the album's Bandcamp site) is obviously tongue in cheek. In Chapter 2, I pointed out that McComb had conflicting emotions about his hometown, which inspired many of his songs. On the surface, the lyrics describe the physical sensations of returning home – the plane descending, the familiar sights and the comfort of being back in a familiar bed. However, the subtext suggests a deeper, more ambiguous emotional experience. The line 'You feel the skin tight against your bones' conveys a sense of constriction and rising tension. It's difficult being a prodigal son. The prospect of having to account for all the things you've done generates anxiety and a self-reflective frame of mind. What will people think of me? What have I achieved while I've been away? Have I lived up to people's expectations? The emotional pressure of having to account for oneself tempers the joy of returning to a familiar place.

Since the song follows 'Lucky for Some' with its image of an infirm narrator staring up at a ceiling fan from his hospital bed, I think it's possible to read the lyrics as a kind of fever dream. The line 'All night long staring at the ceiling/All night long the same damn feeling' connects the two songs in my mind. Perhaps the narrator dreams about returning home during a time of physical and emotional crisis? Either way, the phrase 'such a fine feeling' is repeated ironically, suggesting that the song is not a paean to Perth (despite the references to neat lawns and the river). For me, its tone is closer to songs like 'The Green, Green Grass of Home' or 'Long Black Limousine'. The first song is narrated by a condemned man and the second by a ghost. So, it's possible to detect traces of the eerie in this song, too. The references to green lawns, clean streets and the cool breeze blowing off the river evoke a nostalgia tinged with menace. Home has become unhomely in the Freudian sense. In his oft-cited essay of 1919, Freud defines the uncanny (*das Unheimliche*) as a feeling of unease or eeriness arising when something familiar becomes strange or unsettling. The experience of the uncanny is often linked to repressed fears or childhood memories. This sensation occurs at the boundary between the known and unknown, where repressed material resurfaces unexpectedly (1955, 217–56). In the context of the song, the passage of time has made what was once familiar strange.

Rob Snarski, delivers a typically nuanced performance, which captures the song's unsettling mixture of nostalgia and dread. As good a lyricist as McComb undoubtedly was, it's important to remind ourselves that he was also a musician, constantly searching for the right melody and arrangement to support his words. 'So Good to be Home' offers a compelling illustration of how the musicians transformed a bare-bones cassette demo into something rich in atmosphere and texture. J. P. Shilo's approach in these projects, as he describes it, was akin to the work of a Foley artist in film, sculpting sound to evoke a particular mood: 'I had a concept for the introduction of the song which I play with a slide and an octave shifter with the desire to give the impression of an aeroplane as the lyrics begin with a plane landing' (Personal Interview, 2024).

This haunting, continuous sound merges with Graham Lee's non-melodic pedal steel to form a soundscape that envelops the listener right from the introduction, establishing a mysterious tone that underscores the entire performance.

The band's additional contributions, such as the simple yet evocative guitar riff interspersed between verses, reinforce the atmosphere. This riff, spare but deliberate, calls to mind similar lines from Triffids' classics, particularly the iconic 'Wide Open Road'. It's not just a flourish, but an integral part of the song's overall architecture, offering subtle echoes of the band's past while guiding the listener through the evolving soundscape.

'Look Out for Yourself'

Sung by Alex Gow, 'Look Out for Yourself' is a reflective missive from a lonely place. The lyrics suggest we are condemned to face the final curtain by ourselves, hence the imperative: 'look out for yourself'.

The lyrics of this song are harsh, if you read them on the page. The narrator issues a series of blunt instructions: 'I want you to look around the room you're in/Tell me do you see someone else?' They then implore their interlocutor to 'look out for yourself', because 'nobody else will'. Without the music, it's unclear if the narrator is addressing a friend or talking to themselves.

Alex Gow's sensitive reading of the song gives me the impression that the narrator is engaged in an interior monologue. Gow's voice is restrained. Its tone is almost gentle. There's nothing harsh about his enunciation or phrasing. He's attuned to the song's sentiment. It feels as if the narrator is giving himself a kind of pep talk. The musical accompaniment is unsettling. I hear spooky backing vocals low in the mix, which sometimes blend in with Graham Lee's ethereal pedal steel, and Bruce Haymes' delicate Wurlitzer tones. J. P. Shilo's accordion phrases contribute to the track's otherworldly atmosphere.

Lines like 'Step lightly off the kerb now/There's no-one left to catch your breath' evoke a fragile, precarious state. The metaphor of stepping off a curb suggests a transition or decision fraught with risk, while the absence of someone to 'catch your breath' intensifies the theme of solitude. Psychologically, the narrator is in a liminal space, poised between life and death.

Superficially, the song is about self-reliance and independence, but we can read the line, 'Turn off everything/ Feeding into your veins/Just listen out for the sound you're making' as an injunction to tune out all distractions and focus on one's inner voice. The narrator speaks to himself, willing himself to explore his intuitive creativity ('You've only got one skin to save now'). This reading is reinforced by the line 'Just listen out for the sound you're making' which brings attention to the self in a physical, auditory way. It suggests a turning inward, listening to one's own rhythm, breathing, or voice to ground oneself during a period of uncertainty.

On a more general level, the song poses a series of thoughtful existential questions: what is my purpose in the world? Who will take care of me? Who should I listen to? External sources of knowledge such as other people cannot provide the answers to these questions; the narrator states you need to 'Find out for yourself'.

Gow's performance conveys an undercurrent of care. The painful reality of self-reliance is tempered by the self-confidence that comes out of acting authentically. This mix of detachment and empathy gives the song an emotional complexity that avoids veering into nihilism or despair. The line 'You know how bad it feels when you fake it' directly addresses the emotional toll of inauthenticity, whether in relationships, behaviour or self-presentation. It points to a dissonance between the inner self and external expectations, urging the narrator's interlocutor to shed pretence. Authenticity becomes a path to liberation.

'Make Believe We're Not Here in Hell'

This is a harrowing song about human vulnerability and mortality, which is why it's tempting to read the lyrics autobiographically. McComb was obviously in a precarious state of health when he wrote this song, but, like so many of his personal compositions, this work is more complex than it first appears. The narrator is singing to a friend who is close to death ('You don't recover/Once you've reached this stage'). The narrator can see the life force oozing out of his companion. These lyrics paint a vivid picture of two people navigating an emotional landscape that feels akin to purgatory or hell. They grapple with despair, ageing and an impending sense of loss. So, what to do and where to go when life becomes unbearable? Superficially, the repeated phrase 'make believe' suggests a deliberate choice to embrace fantasy or denial to cope with existential despair. The narrator seems to suggest that even a pretence of joy or love is worth embracing if it can provide temporary solace.

The reference to 'demons in soft focus' and 'the sweetest taste of poison' suggests another, more self-destructive approach to pain relief. The narrator's longing for wine and 'calm waters' evokes a craving for any form of respite. However, we can also read the song as an ode to the power of song: 'Maybe it's time to make believe/And to sing these songs/If it stops the pain'. As I listen to this song, I'm even more convinced that McComb saw songwriting as a spiritual vocation.

Romy Vager turns in a compelling performance. Her voice is plaintive, imbued with a quietly desperate sense of melancholy, as she slowly builds the intensity of her performance. The song works even without the listener having any knowledge of McComb's precarious state of health, but, like the four preceding songs, it shows that his vocation as a songwriter gave him the ability to write about his approaching demise with courage and insight. The instrumentation is sparse, mainly piano, acoustic guitar and Graham Lee's pedal steel. The restrained, stripped-down ensemble playing lends a fragile intimacy to the song.

'This Whole World's about to Slide'

The Triffids often sequenced their most dramatic songs towards the end of their albums. Think of the epic scope of songs like 'Stolen Property' the penultimate song on *Born Sandy Devotional*, or 'Save What You Can' on *Calenture*. Both compositions are a bit like dramatic monologues: a single character conveys a sense of emotional distress in a conversational mode of address. 'This Whole World's about to Slide' belongs to this category of song. The narrator is on the edge of an emotional breakdown; he can hear voices that interrupt his sleep, he's paranoid, distrustful of those around him and haunted by a sense of imminent doom. The entire world, it seems, is poisoned: 'The well you poisoned befalls another/First your friend, and then your brother/Soon you cannot trust one face/Every drink you take might be laced.' While the lyrics suggest the narrator is undergoing some kind of deep personal distress ('Loss of heart and hearth and home'), it is tempting to read the song as a prescient diagnosis of the current state of the world. Indeed, the narrator appears to possess a prophetic ability to see the future; he sees through the soles of his feet that 'the whole world's about to slide'.

The song is suffused with other disturbing, surreal images like the strange thing growing at the back of the narrator's eye as well as, of course, the titular 'Truckload of Sky', which I read as a kind of irresistible force that the narrator needs to hold him down, to stop him drifting away into the void. The repeated line, 'tell me how much lucky I got', feels almost sarcastic, as if the speaker is mocking the notion of luck or fortune in a world that's disintegrating around them. It suggests a longing for some semblance of hope, but also a recognition that luck has perhaps run out. The song reminds me of the predicament of Jesus on the cross in Martin Scorsese's adaptation of *The Last Temptation of Christ*: before experiencing his vivid hallucination, Christ, who like the narrator of McComb's song is paranoid and delusional, looks up at the heavens for a sign of redemption while fearing that he's been forsaken.

Vocally, Simon Breed nails this complex lyric with its emotional twists: 'So tell me, just how lucky I got?' 'Not very' is the obvious response if one pays heed to the suspicious minds and chattering spooks that work their way through this track, sonically and lyrically. This song has grandeur and gravity and is a fitting finale to this extraordinary record.

Bonus Tracks

The CD version of the album contains three bonus tracks that date back to McComb's teenage years. His precocious talent as a songwriter, as these early compositions prove, is clear. The tracks originally appeared on the sixth Triffids tape recorded in 1981 when McComb was nineteen years old (and are available in their original form on the *Come Ride with Me* box set released in 2010). The first two tracks, 'No Desire' and 'Thanks for Everything', sound like forgotten pop treasures from the 1960s. Highlighting the emotions of apathy and detachment from the world and its pressures, the first explores teenage alienation, while the second song exudes sarcasm and a withering sense of irony. In some ways, these re-recordings of three of McComb's teenage compositions are the most unsettling on the album since they show his almost prescient sensibility at work. There is something especially moving about these songs being interpreted by mature singers who act as mediums for McComb's ambitious teenage spirit, which seeps through these performances. The songs show how McComb sought to close the gap between the apparent disposability of pop music and the enduring force of complex lyrics.

'No Desire'

'No Desire' describes a drug overdose, but also paints a picture of someone who has become numb to the world around them, possibly because of medical or psychological intervention, symbolized by the 'blue ones to let you down, red ones to lift you up'. The lines suggest the song's female protagonist is being treated or controlled, but despite this external intervention, they remain unresponsive and detached, with 'no desire'. There are also hints at societal pressures and expectations of normality or emotional response in this following concise turn of phrase: 'the pleasures of the tongue, the pressures of the flesh', from which the subject seems immune. The imagery of angels taking back their halos and lovers not understanding the protagonist's apathy adds a spiritual and personal dimension to the song, reflecting a deeper struggle with identity and existential purpose. The song captures a sense of frustration from both the protagonist and those around her, as she cannot respond to the pleasures or opportunities life offers. This reflection on youth, emotional disconnection, and the consequences of trying to force a response where there is none shows McComb's maturity as a lyricist, which contrasts with the snotty protestations of British punk. Gow's impassioned vocal performance gives the song a compelling intensity befitting of a 'lost' garage rock classic.

'Thanks for Everything'

The narrator of 'Thanks for Everything' could be addressing a parent, sibling, friend, lover or teacher. The lyrics drip with sarcasm and irony, conveying a sense of bitterness about a relationship where one person feels manipulated or patronised. J. P. Shilo's performance underscores the speaker's detached, heavily acerbic tone, expressing 'thanks' for the things the other person has done, but these acknowledgements are obviously hollow, suggesting that the relationship or interaction was not mutually fulfilling. The chorus is withering with its repetition of 'Thanks for Everything', and listing the things done 'for me', including singing songs and winning wars, intensifies the irony. It sounds as though the other person took on an almost saviour-like role, but the speaker didn't find joy or satisfaction in the relationship. 'It's all been too much fun for me' reads as a sarcastic reflection on the experience.

'Somewhere in the Shadows'

The last song on the album is, arguably, the most affecting recording on *Truckload of Sky*. Robert McComb told me,

> 'Somewhere in the Shadows' has always been a song that Dave thought he could recycle one day. And he thought the same about 'Thanks for Everything'. In fact, we heard him rework the rhythm of the song on one of the cassettes we found. He gave it a funky feel, so we took that idea, respecting the fact that this song might have been written in 1979 or thereabouts.
>
> (Personal Interview, 2024)

Sung as a duet by Rob Snarski and Lenore Stephens, the song is about unfulfilled dreams and the impossibility of fulfilling one's desires. Bleddyn Butcher describes the original recording as 'a curious song, a mixture of stolid longing and sour polemic' (2011, 62). Whereas the duet sung by McComb and Margaret Gillard (a member of The Triffids at the time of recording) is rough and somewhat tentative, Snarski and Stephens bring out the composition's spectral qualities.

The imagery of someone 'waiting' in the shadows, only to 'disappear as quickly as they came', reinforces the idea that desire is elusive and deferential. The second verse speaks to the ultimately hopeless balms (lust, alcohol and tranquillisers) people often use to fill the hole created by unrequited love, but the song concludes with a glimmer of hope: 'Somewhere in the shadows/There's an answer to your prayer.' There's still a belief that a metaphysical ideal – a 'knight', a 'maiden' or 'an answer to your prayer' – exists, but remains shrouded in mystery, an intangible spectre in the shadows. These lyrics reflect a deep emotional maturity, touching on many of McComb's favourite themes: elusive fulfilment, transient desires and the constant search for something or someone that could bring solace or metaphysical resolution to the mystery of life. Put differently, this reflection on unattainable dreams and the feeling of being left with 'nothing' adds a layer of poignancy. It's as though McComb, even as a teenager, was in touch with a deeper awareness of life's fragility and the futile search for meaning.

Snarski and Stephens conjure McComb's spirit from the shadows of his music. Their performance provides a fitting coda to an album that consolidates McComb's status as one of the most significant and insightful writers of his generation. By recording his lost songs, the friends of David McComb pay sincere tribute to his indefatigable creative spirit and bestow a precious gift to his fans and admirers.

5 Remember me! David McComb's legacy

Sometimes it's hard to see the contours of a story until it's written. Such has been the case with this book. It occurs to me, now that I've come to the end of this project, that David McComb has much in common with Joseph Campbell's mythic hero.[1] Indeed, his life follows the arc of the hero's journey, up to a point. He starts as a precocious talent, gathers a band of loyal companions and sets off on an adventure. He has a dream, a mission, a vocation, which I've argued is akin to a religious calling. He overcomes obstacles, such as the limitations of a small-town music scene obsessed with cover bands, an indifferent Australian music industry that gives independent bands short shrift, and dubious business deals that keep the band lean and hungry.

Despite these impediments, The Triffids establish a significant following in Europe, record critically acclaimed

---

[1] Joseph Campbell's mythic hero, outlined in *The Hero with a Thousand Faces* (2012), follows a universal journey known as the Hero's Journey, which comprises three main stages: departure, where the hero leaves their ordinary world after receiving a call to adventure; initiation, where they face trials, gain transformative wisdom and achieve a climactic victory; and return, where they bring their newfound knowledge or boon back to their community. McComb didn't achieve a climactic victory, at least not in his lifetime.

albums and sign with Island records, a major music label. And as I mentioned in Chapter 3, the prestigious *NME* pondered whether 1985 was going to be the year of Triffids. Alas, it was not to be. There was to be no 'climactic victory'. McComb and his bandmates could see the brass ring, but it eluded their grasp, and the band broke up in 1989. McComb soldiered on for a while, but eventually returned home by which time musical trends had changed. He kept writing even as his health failed him. He produced some of his best work towards the end of his life, but he left this world with unfinished business. If ghosts exist, then McComb's ghost is hungry, restless, passionate. His phantom is probably chasing the next great song – it will take more than a 'truckload of sky' to hold this spectre down, quell its thirst for the next transcendental tune.

The wheel of fortune turned, and McComb floundered in a sea of troubles in his final years. He left behind, though, a prodigious body of work. Some of it remained buried in his archive until his friends uncovered his lost songs. McComb obviously inspired love and loyalty in those close to him, which brings me back to hauntology. King Hamlet, the most famous ghost in Western literature, exhorts his son, Hamlet, the Prince of Denmark, to 'Remember Me!' Within Shakespeare's play, the ghost's plea for remembrance is not just a personal request but a demand for action: to avenge his wrongful death. Memory, in this context, becomes a moral duty tied to justice, and the ghost is a figure whose existence and story must not fade into oblivion. King Hamlet's ghost embodies the spectral, being neither fully alive nor completely gone. His return disrupts the linearity of time, bringing the past forcefully into the present. This representation of spectrality inspired Derrida's neologism, hauntology and resonates with my reading of *Truckload of Sky*, an album which is an act of remembrance for an artist who died an untimely death.

There is a sense in which the friends of David McComb attempt to set things right by bringing his lost songs into the present and preventing his memory from fading into oblivion. In a way, McComb's quest did not end with his death. His friends have tended to his archive and cared for his legacy in tribute concerts, books, films and now, an album of lost songs. Hauntology addresses unfulfilled promises, but it also speaks to other issues.

In the introduction to this book, I wrote that I've always found The Triffids music haunting. For me, a lot of the band's music is suffused with a distinctive sensibility that is attached to the Western Australia landscape. This is not an especially novel opinion. However, I have used aspects of Mark Fisher's work on hauntological themes, especially his formulation of the eerie and weird, to unpack this aspect of McComb's songwriting and The Triffids' music. The phrase 'Love in Bright Landscapes' sums up McComb's favourite theme, which is why Jonathan Alley used it as the title of his documentary film about McComb and his band. It is also the title of a compilation album by The Triffids. Fisher's concept of the eerie, with its hauntological play of absence and presence, provides a different way of understanding the role of place and space in McComb's work.

As noted in Chapter 1, hauntology, within popular music discourse, is a genre primarily associated with the Ghostbox label. I think this association is restricting and part of this book's aim is to show the concept's relevance for understanding why all recorded music is hauntological. To recap, sound recording literally captures dead voices and facilitates their haunting. And unlike novels and films, most people play their favourite songs and albums again and again. McComb's oeuvre, however, possesses spectral qualities that exceed the boundaries of this general formulation. Existential themes of anxiety, despair, love, loss and mortality are addressed in many of his best songs, including those on *Truckload of Sky*, which were written when McComb was acutely conscious of his impending demise. Songs like 'Lucky for Some' refer directly to his ill health, while others, such as 'So Good to Be Home', take a more oblique approach to the theme of imminent disaster.

As a writer, McComb contributes to Australian culture in a manner that is as significant as any writer of his generation, not least because his work provides a distinctive perspective on Australian life in the 1980s. His lyrics, evocative and poetic, give form to a time that is more complex than its neon-coloured representations suggest.

It is impossible to anticipate what will become of David McComb's legacy. Will a future generation of fans and aspiring songwriters discover his songs and make him another Nick Drake? McComb's reputation has certainly grown in Australia since his death. This is not only because of the quality of his work but also to the persistent, efforts of his friends and fans who refuse to give up the ghost. *Truckload of Sky: The Lost Songs of David McComb, Vol. 1* is the material manifestation of their labour.

References

Abrams, M. H. (1971), *A Glossary of Literary Terms, Third Edition*, New York: Holt, Rinehart and Winston.

Baker, L. (2018), *Rock 'n' Roll Radio: A Case Study of 'Tactics' and Teenage Identity in Perth, WA, 1955–1960*, Perth: Edith Cowan University. Honours Thesis. https://ro.ecu.edu.au/theses_hons/1514.

Barthes, R. (1981), *Camera Lucida*, translated by Richard Howard, New York: Hill and Wang.

Benjamin, W. (1973), 'Art in the Age of Mechanical Reproduction', in H. Arendt ed, H. Zohn, trans. *Illuminations*, 42–53, New York: Schocken Books.

Bennett, A. (2005), 'Introduction: Music, Space and Place', in S. Whiteley, A. Bennett and S. Hawkins, eds, *Music, Space and Place: Popular Music and Cultural Identity*, 1–22, Hampshire: Ashgate Publishing.

Brabazon, T., ed (2005), *Liverpool of the South Seas: Perth and its Popular Music*, Perth: University of Western Australia.

Brault, P. and M. Naas (2001), 'Editors Introduction', in P. Brault and M. Naas, trans. *The Work of Mourning*, Chicago, IL: University of Chicago Press.

Butcher, B. (2011), *Save What You Can: The Day of The Triffids*, Marrickville: Treadwater Press.

Calloway, B. (2006), 'Liner Notes', The Triffids, *In the Pines* (Reissue), Domino Records.

Campbell, J. (2012), *The Hero with a Thousand Faces*, 3rd edition, *The Collected Works of Joseph Campbell*. Novato, CA: New World Library.

Cohen, N. (2000), *Long Steel Rail: The Railroad in American Folksong*, Chicago, IL: University of Illinois Press.

Colebrook, C. (2009), 'The Singularity of The Triffids', in C. Coughran and N. Lucy, eds, *Vagabond Holes: David McComb and The Triffids*, 303–14, Fremantle: Fremantle Press.

Condon, D. (2020), 'The Story of Classic Perth Punks The Victims'. Accessed 20 October 2024. https://www.abc.net.au/listen/doublej/music-reads/features/the-victims-dave-faulkner-james-baker-ray-ahn-television-addict/12592604.

Cooder, Ry (1974), *Paradise and Lunch* [Album] Reprise Records.

Coughran, C. (2009), 'Love in Bright Landscapes: McComb's Lyricism', in C. Coughran, and N. Lucy, eds, *Vagabond Holes: David McComb and The Triffids*, 269–79, Fremantle: Fremantle Press.

Coughran, C. and N. Lucy, eds (2009), *Vagabond Holes: David McComb and The Triffids*, Fremantle: Fremantle Press.

Cull, F. (2005), 'The Wide Open Road – Filling the Potholes', in T. Brabazon, ed, *Liverpool of the South Seas: Perth and Its Popular Music*, 20–8, Crawley: University of Western Australia.

D'Cruz, G. (2015), 'He's Not There: Velvet Goldmine and the Specters of David Bowie', in T. Cinque, C. Moore and S. Redmond, eds, *Enchanting David Bowie: Space/Time/Body/Memory*, 259–73, New York: Bloomsbury Academic.

D'Cruz, G. (2022), *Hauntological Dramaturgy: Affects, Archives Ethics*, Abingdon: Routledge.

D'Cruz, C. and G. D'Cruz (2013), 'Even the Ghost Was More than One Person: Hauntology and Authenticity in Todd Haynes' I'm Not There'. *Film-Philosophy*, 17 (1): 315–30.

Derrida, J. (1994), *Specters of Marx: The State of the Debt, the Work of Mourning, and the New International*, London and New York: Routledge.

Derrida, J. (1996), *Archive Fever, a Freudian Impression*, translated by Eric Prenowitz, Chicago, IL, and London: University of Chicago Press.

Derrida, J. (1997), *The Politics of Friendship*, translated by George Collins, New York: Verso.

Derrida, J. (2001), *The Work of Mourning*, translated by Pascale-Anne Brault and Michael Naas, Chicago, IL: University of Chicago Press.

Dewsbury, R. (1983), 'The Year of The Triffids'. *The West Australian*, February.

Dimery, R. and M. Lydon, eds (2021), *1001 Albums You Must Hear before You Die, Updated Edition*, London: Murdoch Books.

Dwyer, M. (2020), 'David McComb's Legacy Lives on in an Album of "Lost" Songs'. *The Age*, March 27. Accessed 15 October 2024. https://www.theage.com.au/culture/music/david-mccomb-s-legacy-lives-on-in-an-album-of-lost-songs-20200323-p54d1v.html?fbclid=IwY2xjawF5p-NleHRuA2FlbQIxMQAB Ha6SqpgroAx09H1dmoxqZrUy0QMEfwzdlNXN1ssAmOL wB_UjQokn3mzoig_aem_gdGFVJ84Yt3Qfci0srWnfA.

Eliot, T.S. (1932), 'Tradition and the Individual Talent', in *Collected Essays*, 13–22, London: Faber and Faber.

Felski, R. (2015), *The Limits of Critique*, Chicago, IL, and London: The University of Chicago Press.

Fisher, M. (2009), *Capitalist Realism: Is There No Alternative?* Winchester: Zero Books.

Fisher, M. (2012), 'What Is Hauntology'. *Film Quarterly*, 66 (1): 16–24.

Fisher, M. (2014), *Ghosts of My Life: Writings on Depression, Hauntology and Lost Futures*, Winchester: Zero Books.

Fisher, M. (2016), *The Weird and the Eerie*, London: Repeater.

Freud, S. (1955), 'The Uncanny', in *Standard Edition of the Complete Psychological Works*, Vol 17, James Strachey, ed and trans. London: The Hogarth Press.

Frith, S. (1996), *Performing Rites: On the Value of Popular Music*, Cambridge, MA: Harvard University Press.

Galbraith, D. (2019), *Nine Parts Water, One Part Sand: Kim Salmon and the Formula for Grunge*, Melbourne: Melbourne Books.

Gans, H. (1968), 'Urbanism and Suburbanism as Ways of Life: Re-Evaluation of Definitions', in S. F. Fava, ed, *Urbanism in World Perspective: A Reader*, 63–80, New York: Crowell Press.

Gow, A. (2016), 'Q&A with Alex Gow'. *Off The Leash*. Accessed 19 November 2024. https://offtheleash.net.au/features/music/2016/05/qa-alex-gow.

Hägglund, M. (2008), *Radical Atheism: Derrida and the Time of Life*, Stanford, CA: Stanford University Press.

Hawke, S. and M. Gallagher (1989), *Noonkanbah: Whose Land, Whose Law*, Fremantle: Fremantle Arts Centre Press.

Haynes, R. (1999), *Seeking the Centre: The Australian Desert in Literature, Art and Film*, Cambridge: Cambridge University Press.

Heidegger, M. (1962), *Being and Time*, translated by John Macquarrie and Edward Robinson, Oxford: Blackwell.

Howe, R. (1994), 'Inner Suburbs: From Slums to Gentrification', in Louise C. Johnson, ed, *Suburban Dreaming: An Interdisciplinary Approach to Australian Cities*, Geelong: Deakin University Press.

It's Raining Pleasure (2009), [DVD] Dir: Steven Levett, Australia: Madman.

Kakulas, P. (2020), Quoted in 'David McComb–*Truckload of Sky*'. Accessed 16 October 2024. https://thefatangelsings.com/2020/03/12/david-mccomb-truckload-of-sky/.

Kilpin, C. (2005), 'Writing the Perth Music Scene', in T. Brabazon, ed, *Liverpool of the South Seas: Perth and Its Popular Music*, Crawley: University of Western Australia, 138–46.

Kinsella, J. (2009), 'Introduction: In between Words', in *Beautiful Waste: Poems by David McComb*, Chris Coughran and Niall Lucy, eds, Fremantle: Fremantle Press.

Krauth, K. (Host). (2022). 'Wide Open Road by The Triffids and David McComb' (4) [Audio podcast episode]. *Almost a Mirror*. https://podcasts.apple.com/au/podcast/episode-4-wide-open-road-by-the-triffids-david-mccomb/id158650 0703?i=1000551340687.

Lee, G. (2009), 'A Sea of Plastic Daffodils', in C. Coughran and N. Lucy, eds, *Vagabond Holes: David McComb and The Triffids*, 159–62, Fremantle: Fremantle Press.

Lee, G. (2020), 'Liner Notes', in *Truckload of Sky: The Lost Songs of David McComb Vol. 1*, CD, Lost Records and Tapes.

Lee, G. (2023), Facebook Post. Accessed 21 October 2024. https://www.facebook.com/story.php/?story_fbid=74026487144038 0&id=100063706203888.

Lee, G. (2024), 'Personal Interview', 11 April.

Levinas, E. (1969), *Totality and Infinity*, Pittsburgh, PA: Duquesne University Press.

Love in Bright Landscapes. (2021), [Film] Dir: Jonathan Alley, Australia: Atticus Media.

Lucy, N. (2004), *A Derrida Dictionary*, Oxford: Blackwell.

Lucy, N. (2009a), 'Introduction', in C. Coughran and N. Lucy, eds, *Vagabond Holes: David McComb and The Triffids*, 13–17, Fremantle: Fremantle Press.

Lucy, N. (2009b), 'Towards a Minor Music', in C. Coughran and N. Lucy, eds, *Vagabond Holes: David McComb and The Triffids*, 181–94, Fremantle: Fremantle Press.

Marcus, G. (1997), *Invisible Republic: Bob Dylan's Basement Tapes*, New York: Holt.

Marcus, G. (2001), *The Weird Old America*, New York: Picador.

Massumi, B. (2016), 'Working Principles', in Andrew Murphie, ed, *The Go-To How To Book of Anarchiving*, Montréal: The Senselab.

Matzkov, G., ed (2016), *Way Out West: The West Australian Alternative Music Scene 1976–1989*, Fremantle: High Voltage Press.

McComb, D. (1990), 'David McComb Comments on 10 Songs', *JUKE* Magazine, 19 May. https://www.thetriffids.com/juke.shtml. Accessed 20 October 2024.

McComb, D. (1991), [Radio Interview] Interview on Swedish Radio: 23 June 1991.

McComb, D. (1993), [Radio Interview] 3SER Casey Radio, Melbourne.

McComb, D. (1994), 'Biography'. [Publicity Press Kit], Melbourne: Mushroom Records.

McComb, D. (1995), 'Love of Will Press Kit', Mushroom Records.

McComb, D. (2009), *Beautiful Waste: Poems by David McComb*, C. Coughran and N. Lucy, eds, Fremantle: Fremantle Press.

McComb, R. (2024), 'Personal Interview', 11 April.

McGowan, A. (2009), 'Jesus Calling: Religion in the Songs of David McComb', in C. Coughran and N. Lucy, eds, *Vagabond Holes: David McComb and The Triffids*, 117–27, Fremantle: Fremantle Press.

Murray, L. A. (1989), *The Vernacular Republic: Poems, 1961–83*, Sydney: Angus and Robertson.

Neates, W. (2006), 'The Days of The Triffids: A Retrospective with Graham Lee and Rob McComb', *Perfect Sound Forever*.

Accessed 15 October 2024. https://www.furious.com/perfect/triffids.html.

Newman, P. (2016), 'Perth as a "Big" City: Reflections on Urban Growth', *Thesis Eleven*, 135 (1): 139–51.

Nichols, D. (2009), 'Wow and Flutter', in C. Coughran and N. Lucy, eds, *Vagabond Holes: David McComb and The Triffids*, 79–91, Fremantle: Fremantle Press.

Nietzsche, F. (1967), *The Birth of Tragedy and The Case of Wagner*, translated by Walter Kaufmann, New York: Vintage Books.

Panizza, A. and J. Stratton (2019), 'Into the Groove: Experiencing Difference in the Perth Nightclub Scene of the 1980s', *Social Identities: Journal for the Study of Race, Nation and Culture*, 25 (5): 714–23.

Pierre, D.B.C. (2009), 'Farewell from the Wharf of Innocence', in C. Coughran and N. Lucy, eds, *Vagabond Holes: David McComb and The Triffids*, 329–31, Fremantle: Fremantle Press.

Reid, G. (2023), 'David McComb of The Triffids, Interviewed (1994): Here… and Gone Too Soon'. https://www.elsewhere.co.nz/absoluteelsewhere/10881/david-mccomb-of-the-triffids-interviewed-1994-here--and-gone-too-soon/.

Reynolds, S. (2012), *Retromania: Pop Culture's Addiction to its Own Past*, London: Faber and Faber.

Roms, H. (2013), 'Archiving Legacies: Who Cares for Performance Remains', in G. Borggreen and R. Gade, eds, *Performing Archives/Archives of Performance*, 35–52, Copenhagen: Museum Tusculanum Press.

Ryan, M. (1985), 'The Path of Least Resistance', *RAM*, January 4.

Sacks, O. (2008), *Musicophilia: Tales of Music and the Brain*, London: Picador.

Shilo, J. P. (2024), Personal Interview, 17 September.

Sisson, A. and P. J. Maggin (2018), '"Reclaiming Northbridge": Urban (Dis)Order and Territorial Stigmatisation in Perth's Night Time Economy precinct', *Urban Policy and Research*, 36: 123–37.

Snarski, R. (2017), *You're Not Rob Snarski: Crumbs from the Cake*, Crawley: University of Western Australia Publishing.

Snow, M. (1986), 'Review of Born Sandy Devotional', *New Musical Express*, 21 June.

Stevenson, R. W. (1997), *Modernist Fiction: An Introduction*, London and New York: Routledge.

Stratton, J. (1992), *The Young Ones: Working Class Culture, Consumption and the Category of Youth*, Perth: Black Swan Press.

Stratton, J. (2005), 'Pissed on Another Planet: The Perth Sound of the '70s and '80s', *Perfect Beat: The Pacific Journal for Research into Contemporary Music and Popular Culture*, 7 (2): 36–60.

Stratton, J. (2007), 'The Triffids: The Sense of a Place', *Popular Music and Society*, 30 (3): 377–99.

Stratton, J. (2009), 'Suburban Stories: Dave McComb and the Perth Experience', in C. Coughran and N. Lucy, eds, *Vagabond Holes: David McComb and The Triffids*, 35–43, Fremantle: Fremantle Press.

Stratton, J. and A. Trainer (2016), 'Nothing Happens Here: Songs about Perth', *Thesis Eleven*, 135 (1): 34–50.

Sweeting, A. (1986), 'Review of *Born Sandy Devotional*', *The Guardian*, 30 May.

Tavis, A. (1993), 'Russia in Rilke: Rainer Maria Rilke's
Correspondence with Marina Tsvetaeva', *Slavic Review*, 52 (3):
494–511.

Trainer, A. (2016), 'Perth Punk and the Construction of Urbanity in
a Suburban City', *Popular Music*, 35 (1): 100–17.

Tompkin, J.G. (2012), 'New Frequencies from Planet Perth: Punk
Rock and Western Australia's Sesquicentenary Celebrations'.
Master of Creative Arts Thesis. Perth: Curtin University.

The Triffids. (1984), *Raining Pleasure* [Album] Hot Records.

The Triffids. (1987), *Calenture*, [Vinyl Album] Island Records.

Tsvetaeva, M. (2009), 'New Year's Letter', in *Bride of Ice: Selected
Poems*, E. Feinstein, trans. Manchester: Carcanet Press.

Turner, G. (1992), 'Australian Popular Music and Its Contexts', in
P. Hayward, ed, *From Pop to Punk to Postmodernism: Popular
Music and Australian Culture from the 1960s to the 1990s*, 11–24,
North Sydney: Allen & Unwin.

Walker, C. (1996), *Stranded: The Secret History of Australian
Independent Music 1977–1991*, Sydney: Pan Macmillan.

Walker, C. (2021), *Stranded: Australian Independent Music, 1976–
1992 Revised and Expanded Edition*, The Visible Spectrum.

Walker, C. (2023), *Inner City Sound: Punk and Post-Punk in Australia,
1976–1985*, Portland, OR: Verse Chorus Press.

Weir, W. L. (2023), *BBC Radiophonic Workshop: A Retrospective*,
New York and London: Bloomsbury Academic.

Weisbard, E. (1994), 'A Simple Song That Lives Beyond Time',
The New York Times, November 13.

Wilde, O. (2003), 'Preface', *The Picture of Dorian Gray*, London:
Penguin Classics.

Whish-Wilson, D. (2013), *Perth*, Sydney: Newsouth Books.

Wilson, C. (2014), *Let's Talk About Love: Why Other People Have Such Bad Taste*, New York and London: Bloomsbury Academic.

Wilson, N. (2009), 'McComb's Ambivalent Romanticism', in C. Coughran and N. Lucy, eds, *Vagabond Holes: David McComb and The Triffids*, 245–64, Fremantle: Fremantle Press.